Upgrading to Microsoft® Office 2007

ILLUSTRATED

BRIEF

Barbara Clemens/MT Cozzola/
Barbara Waxer

THOMSON

COURSE TECHNOLOGY

Australia • Canada • Mexico • Singapore • Spain • United Kingdom • United States

THOMSON

COURSE TECHNOLOGY

Upgrading to Microsoft® Office 2007—Illustrated Brief
Barbara Clemens / MT Cozzola / Barbara Waxer

Senior Acquisitions Editor:
Marjorie Hunt

Senior Product Manager:
Karen Stevens

Associate Product Manager:
Rebecca Padrick

Editorial Assistant:
Michelle Camisa

Senior Marketing Manager:
Joy Stark

Marketing Coordinator:
Jennifer Hankin

Contributing Authors:
Elizabeth Eisner Reding, Lisa Ruffolo

Developmental Editors:
Barbara Clemens, MT Cozzola,
Lisa Ruffolo, Barbara Waxer

Production Editors:
Philippa Lehar, Marisa Taylor (GEX
Publishing Services)

Copy Editor:
GEX Publishing Services

Proofreader:
GEX Publishing Services

Indexer:
GEX Publishing Services

QA Manuscript Reviewers:
John Freitas, Jeff Schwartz, Susan
Whalen

Cover Designers:
Elizabeth Paquin, Kathleen Fivel

Cover Artist:
Mark Hunt

Composition:
GEX Publishing Services

About This Book

Welcome to the *Upgrading Guide to Microsoft Office 2007—Illustrated Brief*! Since the first book in the Illustrated Series was published in 1994, millions of students have used various Illustrated texts to master software skills and learn computer concepts. We are proud to bring you this new Illustrated book on the most exciting version of Microsoft Office ever to release.

As you probably have heard by now, Microsoft completely redesigned this latest version of Office from the ground up. No more menus! No more toolbars! The software changes Microsoft made were based on years of research during which they studied users' needs and work habits. The result is a phenomenal and powerful new version of the software that will make you and your students more productive and help you get better results faster.

This unique book offers a perfect training solution for experienced Office 2003 users who need to get up to speed quickly on Office 2007. The book focuses on what's new in the software, so that experienced users can quickly get oriented and start being productive using Office 2007. In addition to providing step by step lessons that cover the new features, the end of unit material provides exercises to reinforce skills. The end of the book also includes an Upgrading Command Reference that provides steps for performing tasks in both Office 2003 and Office 2007.

Advisory Board

We thank our Office 2007 Advisory Board who enthusiastically gave us their opinions and helped direct many of the design and pedagogical decisions we made in the development of this book. They are:

Kristen Callahan, Mercer County Community College

Paulette Comet, Assistant Professor, Community College of Baltimore County

Barbara Comfort, J. Sargeant Reynolds Community College

Margaret Cooksey, Tallahassee Community College

Rachelle Hall, Glendale Community College

Hazel Kates, Miami Dade College

Charles Lupico, Thomas Nelson Community College

Author Acknowledgments

Barbara Clemens Many thanks to Marjorie Hunt and Karen Stevens for their skillful project guidance. A big thank you to Lisa Ruffolo, for her patience and her amazing editing skills that helped shape the chapter. And special thanks to my husband, Bill Wiley, for his endless support and good humor.

MT Cozzola My thanks to Lisa, Barbara C., and the incomparable Barbara W.; what a team! A special thanks to Marjorie for providing the opportunity, and to Karen, Marisa, and our friends in MQA for making it all go so smoothly.

Lisa Ruffolo Many thanks to the entire Upgrading to Microsoft Office 2007 team, especially Barbara Clemens for her thoughtful editing and constant encouragement and my co-authors for their foresight and creativity.

Barbara Waxer Great appreciation to an amazing and generous authoring team. My thanks to Lisa and Barbara C., and as always to the inimitable MT Cozzola. Kudos to Marjorie Hunt, Karen Stevens, Marisa Taylor and the MQA team for instilling such high quality in this project.

Preface

Welcome to *Upgrading to Microsoft Office 2007—Illustrated Brief*. If this is your first experience with the Illustrated series, you'll see that this book has a unique design: each skill is presented on two facing pages, with steps on the left and screens on the right. The layout makes it easy to digest a skill without having to read a lot of text and flip pages to see an illustration. The design also makes this a great reference after the course is over! See the illustration on the right to learn more about the pedagogical and design elements of a typical lesson.

This book is an ideal learning tool for experienced Office 2003 users who need to get up and running quickly on Office 2007.

What's in This Book

This book is designed to help Office 2003 users get started using Microsoft Office 2007 quickly. Here are some highlights:

- **Getting Started with Microsoft® Office 2007 Unit**—This unit begins the book and gets students up to speed on features of Office 2007 that are common to all the applications, such as the Ribbon, the Office button, and the Quick Access toolbar.
- **Word Unit**—The Word unit introduces students to the most exciting new features and improvements in Word 2007. Some of the features covered include Quick Styles, themes, table styles, picture styles, margin presets, SmartArt diagrams, Quick Parts and Building Blocks, footnotes, citations and bibliographies, research and translation tools, the Compatibility Checker, and file distribution options.

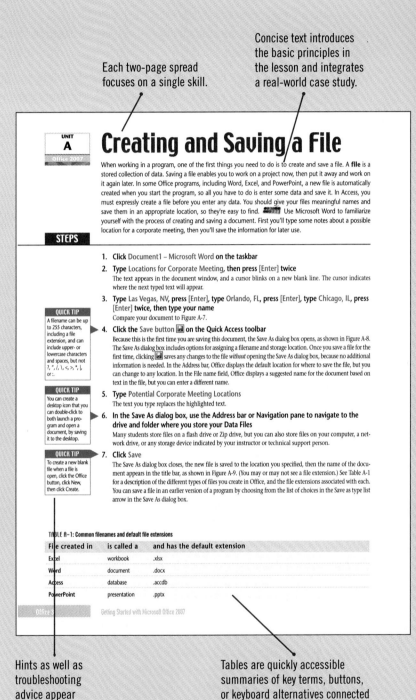

Each two-page spread focuses on a single skill.

Concise text introduces the basic principles in the lesson and integrates a real-world case study.

Hints as well as troubleshooting advice appear right where you need them—next to the step itself.

Tables are quickly accessible summaries of key terms, buttons, or keyboard alternatives connected with the lesson material. Students can refer easily to this information when working on their own projects at a later time.

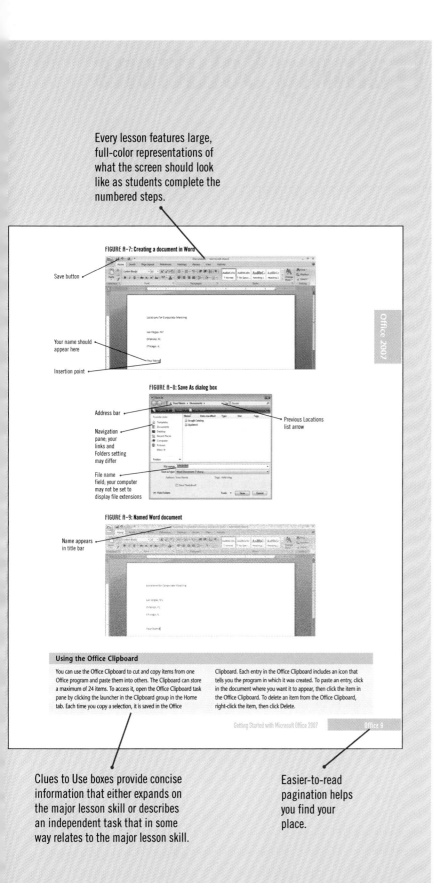

Every lesson features large, full-color representations of what the screen should look like as students complete the numbered steps.

FIGURE A-7: Creating a document in Word

Save button

Your name should appear here

Insertion point

FIGURE A-8: Save As dialog box

Address bar

Navigation pane; your links and Folders setting may differ

File name field; your computer may not be set to display file extensions

Previous Locations list arrow

FIGURE A-9: Named Word document

Name appears in title bar

Office 2007

Using the Office Clipboard

You can use the Office Clipboard to cut and copy items from one Office program and paste them into others. The Clipboard can store a maximum of 24 items. To access it, open the Office Clipboard task pane by clicking the launcher in the Clipboard group in the Home tab. Each time you copy a selection, it is saved in the Office Clipboard. Each entry in the Office Clipboard includes an icon that tells you the program in which it was created. To paste an entry, click in the document where you want it to appear, then click the item in the Office Clipboard. To delete an item from the Office Clipboard, right-click the item, then click Delete.

Clues to Use boxes provide concise information that either expands on the major lesson skill or describes an independent task that in some way relates to the major lesson skill.

Easier-to-read pagination helps you find your place.

- **Excel Unit**—The Excel unit gives students hands-on experience in using the new Excel user interface, including the new themes and styles and the new Page Layout view. It covers the new chart styles and the expanded conditional formatting options. Students type functions using the expanded Function AutoComplete feature and learn about the new Name Manager dialog box. New table (formerly list) features and styles help students create and analyze data, including structured references to speed table calculations. Students explore data relationships using the new PivotTable and PivotChart interface.

- **Access Unit**—The Access Unit introduces students to the new features in Microsoft Office Access 2007 including the Getting Started with Microsoft Office Access page, which provides database templates that students can use immediately to store and track their data; a Navigation Pane that replaces the database window and provides easy access to all of the student's database objects; and the Layout View, which lets students make design changes to forms and reports while their data is displayed.

- **PowerPoint Unit**—PowerPoint 2007 successfully combines its reliable slide-show features with new outstanding graphic capabilities. In this unit, students will become familiar with the new interface, apply many themes and styles to the presentation and to individual elements, create SmartArt graphics, enhance photographs, tables, and charts, and view the slide show in different ways.

Assignments

The assignments on the light purple pages at the end of each unit provide additional hands-on reinforcement in learning Office 2007 skills. Assignments include:

- **Concepts Reviews** consist of multiple choice, matching, and screen identification questions.

- **Skills Reviews** provide additional hands-on, step-by-step reinforcement.

- **Visual Workshops** are practical, self-graded capstone projects that require independent problem solving.

Assessment & Training Solutions

SAM 2007 helps bridge the gap between the classroom and the real world by allowing students to train and test on important computer skills in an active, hands-on environment.

SAM 2007's easy-to-use system includes powerful interactive exams, training, or projects on critical applications such as Word, Excel, Access, PowerPoint, Outlook, Windows, the Internet, and much more. SAM simulates the application environment, allowing students to demonstrate their knowledge and think through the skills by performing real-world tasks.

Designed to be used with the Illustrated series, SAM 2007 includes built-in page references so students can print helpful study guides that match the Illustrated textbooks used in class. Powerful administrative options allow instructors to schedule exams and assignments, secure tests, and run reports with almost limitless flexibility.

A GUIDED TOUR OF MICROSOFT OFFICE 2007, WINDOWS VISTA EDITION

This CD of movie tutorials helps students get exposed to the new features of Microsoft Office 2007 quickly. Dynamic and engaging author Corinne Hoisington presents the highlights of the new features of Word, Excel, Access, and PowerPoint plus a bonus movie tutorial on Windows Vista. This CD is a great supplement to this book, offering a fun overview of the software to inspire students and show them what is possible.

Instructor Resources

The Instructor Resources CD is Thomson Course Technology's way of putting the resources and information needed to teach and learn effectively into your hands. With an integrated array of teaching and learning tools that offer you and your students a broad range of technology-based instructional options, we believe this CD represents the highest quality and most cutting edge resources available to instructors today. Many of these resources are available at *www.course.com*. The resources available with this book are:

- **Instructor's Manual**—Available as an electronic file, the Instructor's Manual includes detailed lecture topics with teaching tips for each unit.

- **Sample Syllabus**—Prepare and customize your course easily using this sample course outline.

- **PowerPoint Presentations**—Each unit has a corresponding PowerPoint presentation that you can use in lecture, distribute to your students, or customize to suit your course.

- **Figure Files**—The figures in the text are provided on the Instructor Resources CD to help you illustrate key topics or concepts. You can create traditional overhead transparencies by printing the figure files. Or you can create electronic slide shows by using the figures in a presentation program such as PowerPoint.

- **Solutions to Exercises**—Solutions to Exercises contains every file students are asked to create or modify in the lessons and end-of-unit material. Also provided in this section, there is a document outlining the solutions for the end-of-unit Concepts Review, Skills Review, and Independent Challenges.

- **Data Files for Students**—To complete most of the units in this book, your students will need Data Files. You can post the Data Files on a file server for students to copy. The Data Files are available on the Instructor Resources CD, the Review Pack, and can also be downloaded from *www.course.com*. In this edition, we have included a lesson on downloading the Data Files for this book, see page xvi.

Instruct students to use the Data Files List included on the Review Pack and the Instructor Resources CD. This list gives instructions on copying and organizing files.

- **ExamView**—ExamView is a powerful testing software package that allows you to create and administer printed, computer (LAN-based), and Internet exams. ExamView includes hundreds of questions that correspond to the topics covered in this text, enabling students to generate detailed study guides that include page references for further review. The computer-based and Internet testing components allow students to take exams at their computers, and also saves you time by grading each exam automatically.

CourseCasts—Learning on the Go. Always Available...Always Relevant.

Want to keep up with the latest technology trends relevant to you? Visit our site to find a library of podcasts, CourseCasts, featuring a "CourseCast of the Week," and download them to your mp3 player at *http://coursecasts.course.com*.

Our fast-paced world is driven by technology. You know because you're an active participant—always on the go, always keeping up with technological trends, and always learning new ways to embrace technology to power your life.

Ken Baldauf, a faculty member of the Florida State University Computer Science Department, is responsible for teaching technology classes to thousands of FSU students each year. He knows what you know; he knows what you want to learn. He's also an expert in the latest technology and will sort through and aggregate the most pertinent news and information so you can spend your time enjoying technology, rather than trying to figure it out.

Visit us at *http://coursecasts.course.com* to learn on the go!

Brief Contents

Contents

Read This Before You Begin

Frequently Asked Questions

What are Data Files?

A Data File is a partially completed Word document, Access database, or another type of file that you use to complete the steps in the units and exercises in order to create the final document that you submit to your instructor. Each unit opener page lists the Data Files that you need for that unit.

Where are the Data Files?

Your instructor will provide the Data Files to you or direct you to a location on a network drive where you can download them. Alternatively, you can follow the instructions on page xvi to download the Data Files from this book's Web page.

What software was used to write and test this book?

This book was written and tested using a typical installation of Microsoft Office 2007 installed on a computer with a typical installation of Microsoft Windows Vista. The browser used for any steps that require a browser is Internet Explorer 7.

If you are using this book on Windows XP, please see the "Important Notes for Windows XP Users" on the next page. If you are using this book on Windows Vista, please see the appendix at the end of this book.

Do I need to be connected to the Internet to complete the steps and exercises in this book?

Some of the exercises in this book assume that your computer is connected to the Internet. If you are not connected to the Internet, see your instructor for information on how to complete the exercises.

What do I do if my screen is different from the figures shown in this book?

This book was written and tested on computers with monitors set at a resolution of 1024 × 768. If your screen shows more or less information than the figures in the book, your monitor is probably set at a higher or lower resolution. If you don't see something on your screen, you might have to scroll down or up to see the object identified in the figures.

The Ribbon (the blue area at the top of the screen) in Microsoft Office 2007 adapts to different resolutions. If your monitor is set at a lower resolution than 1024 × 768, you might not see all of the buttons shown in the figures. The groups of buttons will always appear, but the entire group might be condensed into a single button that you need to click to access the buttons described in the instructions. For example, the figures and steps in this book assume that the Editing group on the Home tab in Word looks like the following:

If your resolution is set to 800 × 600, the Ribbon in Word will look like the following figure, and you will need to click the Editing button to access the buttons that are visible in the Editing group.

1024 × 768 Editing Group

Editing Group on the Home Tab of the Ribbon at 1024 × 768

800 × 600 Editing Group

Editing Group on the Home Tab of the Ribbon at 800 × 600

800 × 600 Editing Group Clicked

Editing Group on the Home Tab of the Ribbon at 800 × 600 is selected to show available buttons

Important Notes for Windows XP Users

The screen shots in this book show Microsoft Office 2007 running on Windows Vista. However, if you are using Microsoft Windows XP, you can still use this book because Office 2007 runs virtually the same on both platforms. There are a few differences that you will encounter if you are using Windows XP. Read this section to understand the differences.

Dialog boxes

If you are a Windows XP user, dialog boxes shown in this book will look slightly different than what you see on your screen. Dialog boxes for Windows XP have a blue title bar, instead of a gray title bar. However, beyond this difference in appearance, the options in the dialog boxes across platforms are the same. For instance, the screen shots below show the Font dialog box running on Windows XP and the Font dialog box running on Windows Vista.

FIGURE 1: Dialog box in Windows XP

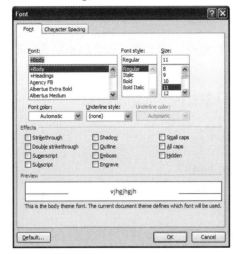

FIGURE 2: Dialog box in Windows Vista

Alternate Steps for Windows XP Users

Nearly all of the steps in this book work exactly the same for Windows XP users. However, there are a few tasks that will require you to complete slightly different steps. This section provides alternate steps for a few specific skills.

Starting a program

1. Click the **Start button** on the taskbar
2. Point to **All Programs**, point to **Microsoft Office**, then click the application you want to use

FIGURE 3: Starting a program

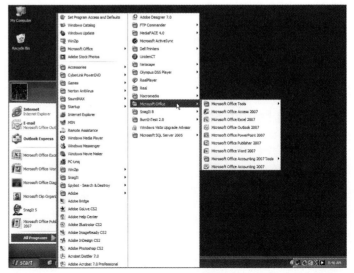

Saving a file for the first time

1. Click the **Office button**, then click **Save As**
2. Type a name for your file in the File name text box
3. Click the **Save in list arrow**, then navigate to the drive and folder where you store your Data Files
4. Click **Save**

FIGURE 4: Save As dialog box

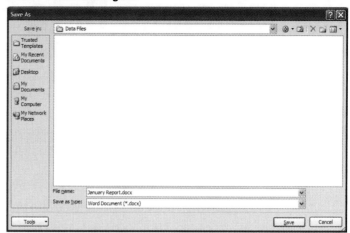

Opening a file

1. Click the **Office button**, then click **Open**
2. Click the **Look in list arrow**, then navigate to the drive and folder where you store your Data Files
3. Click the file you want to open
4. Click **Open**

FIGURE 5: Open dialog box

Downloading Data Files for This Book

In order to complete many of the lesson steps and exercises in this book, you are asked to open and save Data Files. A **Data File** is a partially completed Word document, Access database, or another type of file that you use as a starting point to complete the steps in the units and exercises. The benefit of using a Data File is that it saves you the time and effort needed to create a file; you can simply open a Data File, save it with a new name (so the original file remains intact), then make changes to it to complete lesson steps or an exercise. Your instructor will provide the Data Files to you or direct you to a location on a network drive from which you can download them. Alternatively, you can follow the instructions in this lesson to download the Data Files from this book's Web page.

1. Start Internet Explorer, type www.course.com in the address bar, then press [Enter]

2. When the Course.com Web site opens, click the Student Downloads link

3. On the Student Downloads page, click in the Search text box, type this book's ISBN, 9781423925668, then click Go

QUICK TIP
You can also click Student Downloads on the right side of the product page.

4. When the page opens for this textbook, in the left navigation bar, click the Download Student Files link, then, on the Student Downloads page, click the Data Files link

5. If the File Download – Security Warning dialog box opens, click Save. (If no dialog box appears, skip this step and go to Step 6)

TROUBLE
If a dialog box opens telling you that the download is complete, click Close.

6. If the Save As dialog box opens, click the Save in list arrow at the top of the dialog box, select a folder on your USB drive or hard disk to download the file to, then click Save

7. Close Internet Explorer and then open My Computer or Windows Explorer and display the contents of the drive and folder to which you downloaded the file

8. Double-click the file 925668.exe in the drive or folder, then, if the Open File – Security Warning dialog box opens, click Run

QUICK TIP
By default, the files will extract to C:\ CourseTechnology\ 925668

9. In the WinZip Self-Extractor window, navigate to the drive and folder where you want to unzip the files to, then click Unzip

10. When the WinZip Self-Extractor displays a dialog box listing the number of files that have unzipped successfully, click OK, click Close in the WinZip Self-Extractor dialog box, then close Windows Explorer or My Computer

You are now ready to open the required files.

Getting Started with Microsoft Office 2007

Microsoft Office 2007 is a group of software programs designed to help you create documents, collaborate with co-workers, and track and analyze information. Each program is designed so you can work quickly and efficiently to create professional-looking results. You use different Office programs to accomplish specific tasks, such as writing a letter or producing a sales presentation, yet all the programs have a similar look and feel. Once you become familiar with one program, you'll find it easy to transfer your knowledge to the others. This unit introduces you to the most frequently used programs in Office, as well as common features they all share.

OBJECTIVES

Understand the Office 2007 Suite

Start and exit an Office program

View the Office 2007 user interface

Create and save a file

Open a file and save it with a new name

View and print your work

Get Help and close a file

Understanding the Office 2007 Suite

Microsoft Office 2007 features an intuitive, context-sensitive user interface, so you can get up to speed faster and use advanced features with greater ease. The programs in Office are bundled together in a group called a **suite** (although you can also purchase them separately). The Office suite is available in several configurations, but all include Word and Excel. Other configurations include PowerPoint, Access, Outlook, Publisher, and/or others. Each program in Office is best suited for completing specific types of tasks, though there is some overlap in terms of their capabilities.

DETAILS

The Office programs covered in this book include:

- **Microsoft Office Word 2007**

  When you need to create any kind of text-based document, such as memos, newsletters, or multi-page reports, Word is the program to use. You can easily make your documents look great by inserting eye-catching graphics and using formatting tools such as themes. **Themes** are predesigned combinations of color and formatting attributes you can apply, and are available in most Office programs. The Word document shown in Figure A-1 was formatted with the Solstice theme.

- **Microsoft Office Excel 2007**

  Excel is the perfect solution when you need to work with numeric values and make calculations. It puts the power of formulas, functions, charts, and other analytical tools into the hands of every user, so you can analyze sales projections, figure out loan payments, and present your findings in style. The Excel worksheet shown in Figure A-1 tracks personal expenses. Because Excel automatically recalculates results whenever a value changes, the information is always up-to-date. A chart illustrates how the monthly expenses are broken down.

- **Microsoft Office PowerPoint 2007**

  Using PowerPoint, it's easy to create powerful presentations complete with graphics, transitions, and even a soundtrack. Using professionally designed themes and clip art, you can quickly and easily create dynamic slideshows such as the one shown in Figure A-1.

- **Microsoft Office Access 2007**

  Access helps you keep track of large amounts of quantitative data, such as product inventories or employee records. The form shown in Figure A-1 was created for a grocery store inventory database. Employees use the form to enter data about each item. Using Access enables employees to quickly find specific information such as price and quantity, without hunting through store shelves and stockrooms.

Microsoft Office has benefits beyond the power of each program, including:

- **Common user interface: Improving business processes**

  Because the Office suite programs have a similar **interface**, or look and feel, your experience using one program's tools makes it easy to learn those in the other programs. Office documents are **compatible** with one another, meaning that you can easily incorporate, or **integrate**, an Excel chart into a PowerPoint slide, or an Access table into a Word document.

- **Collaboration: Simplifying how people work together**

  Office recognizes the way people do business today, and supports the emphasis on communication and knowledge-sharing within companies and across the globe. All Office programs include the capability to incorporate feedback—called **online collaboration**—across the Internet or a company network.

FIGURE A-1: Microsoft Office 2007 documents

Word document

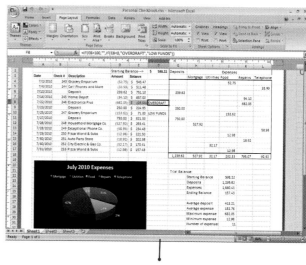

Excel worksheet

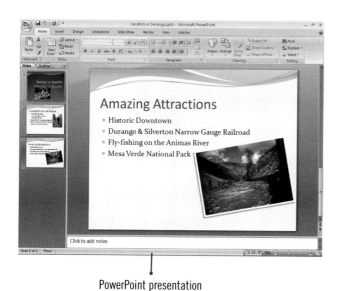

PowerPoint presentation

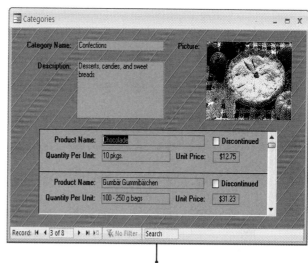

Access database form

Deciding which program to use

Every Office program includes tools that go far beyond what you might expect. For example, although Excel is primarily designed for making calculations, you can use it to create a database. So when you're planning a project, how do you decide which Office program to use? The general rule of thumb is to use the program best suited for your intended task, and make use of supporting tools in the program if you need them. Word is best for creating text-based documents, Excel is best for making mathematical calculations, PowerPoint is best for preparing presentations, and Access is best for managing quantitative data. Although the capabilities of Office are so vast that you *could* create an inventory in Excel or a budget in Word, you'll find greater flexibility and efficiency by using the program designed for the task. And remember, you can always create a file in one program, and then insert it in a document in another program when you need to, such as including sales projections (Excel) in a memo (Word).

Starting and Exiting an Office Program

The first step in using an Office program is of course to open, or **launch**, it on your computer. You have a few choices for how to launch a program, but the easiest way is to click the Start button on the Windows taskbar, or to double-click an icon on your desktop. You can have multiple programs open on your computer simultaneously, and you can move between open programs by clicking the desired program or document button on the taskbar or by using the [Alt][Tab] keyboard shortcut combination. 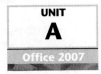 When working, you'll often want to open multiple programs in Office, and switch among them throughout the day. Begin by launching a few Office programs now.

STEPS

QUICK TIP
You can also launch a program by double-clicking a desktop icon or clicking an entry on the Recent Items menu.

1. **Click the Start button ⊕ on the taskbar**

   The Start menu opens, as shown in Figure A-2. If the taskbar is hidden, you can display it by pointing to the bottom of the screen. Depending on your taskbar property settings, the taskbar may be displayed at all times, or only when you point to that area of the screen. For more information, or to change your taskbar properties, consult your instructor or technical support person.

2. **Point to All Programs, click Microsoft Office, then click Microsoft Office Word 2007**

   Microsoft Office Word 2007 starts and the program window opens on your screen.

QUICK TIP
It is not necessary to close one program before opening another.

3. **Click ⊕ on the taskbar, point to All Programs, click Microsoft Office, then click Microsoft Office Excel 2007**

   Microsoft Office Excel 2007 starts and the program window opens, as shown in Figure A-3. Word is no longer visible, but it remains open. The taskbar displays a button for each open program and document. Because this Excel document is **active**, or in front and available, the Microsoft Excel – Book1 button on the taskbar appears in a darker shade.

4. **Click Document1 – Microsoft Word on the taskbar**

   Clicking a button on the taskbar activates that program and document. The Word program window is now in front, and the Document1 – Microsoft Word taskbar button appears shaded.

QUICK TIP
If there isn't room on your taskbar to display the entire name of each button, you can point to any button to see the full name in a Screentip.

5. **Click ⊕ on the taskbar, point to All Programs, click Microsoft Office, then click Microsoft Office PowerPoint 2007**

   Microsoft Office PowerPoint 2007 starts, and becomes the active program.

6. **Click Microsoft Excel – Book1 on the taskbar**

   Excel is now the active program.

QUICK TIP
As you work in Windows, your computer adapts to your activities. You may notice that after clicking the Start button, the name of the program you want to open appears in the Start menu; if so, you can click it to start the program.

7. **Click ⊕ on the taskbar, point to All Programs, click Microsoft Office, then click Microsoft Office Access 2007**

   Microsoft Office Access 2007 starts, and becomes the active program.

8. **Point to the taskbar to display it, if necessary**

   Four Office programs are open simultaneously.

9. **Click the Office button ⊕, then click Exit Access, as shown in Figure A-4**

   Access closes, leaving Excel active and Word and PowerPoint open.

FIGURE A-2: Start menu

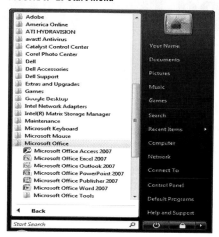

FIGURE A-3: Excel program window and Windows taskbar

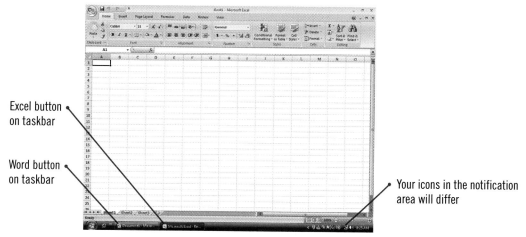

Excel button on taskbar

Word button on taskbar

Your icons in the notification area will differ

FIGURE A-4: Exiting Microsoft Office Access

Microsoft Office button

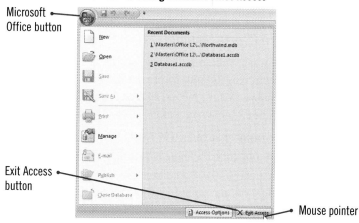

Exit Access button

Mouse pointer

Using shortcut keys to move between Office programs

As an alternative to the Windows taskbar, you can use a keyboard shortcut to move among open Office programs. The [Alt][Tab] keyboard combination lets you either switch quickly to the next open program, or choose one from a palette. To switch immediately to the next open program, press [Alt][Tab]. To choose from all open programs, press and hold [Alt], then press and release [Tab] without releasing [Alt]. A palette opens on screen, displaying the icon and filename of each open program and file. Each time you press [Tab] while holding [Alt], the selection cycles to the next open file. Release [Alt] when the program/file you want to activate is selected.

Viewing the Office 2007 User Interface

One of the benefits of using Office is that the programs have much in common, making them easy to learn and making it simple to move from one to another. Individual Office programs have always shared many features, but the innovations in the Office 2007 user interface mean even greater similarity among them all. That means you can also use your knowledge of one program to get up to speed in another. A **user interface** is a collective term for all the ways you interact with a software program. The user interface in Office 2007 includes a more intuitive way of choosing commands, working with files, and navigating in the program window. Familiarize yourself with some of the common interface elements in Office by examining the PowerPoint program window.

STEPS

QUICK TIP

In addition to the standard tabs on the ribbon, **contextual tabs** open when needed to complete a specific task; they appear in an accent color, and close when no longer needed.

1. **Click Microsoft PowerPoint – [Presentation1] on the taskbar**

   PowerPoint becomes the active program. Refer to Figure A-5 to identify common elements of the Office user interface. The **document window** occupies most of the screen. In PowerPoint, a blank slide appears in the document window, so you can build your slide show. At the top of every Office program window is a **title bar**, which displays the document and program name. Below the title bar is the **Ribbon**, which displays commands you're likely to need for the current task. Commands are organized into **tabs**. The tab names appear at the top of the Ribbon, and the active tab appears in front with its name highlighted. The Ribbon in every Office program includes tabs specific to the program, but all include a Home tab on the far left, for the most popular tasks in that program.

2. **Click the Office button**

   The Office menu opens. This menu contains commands common to most Office programs, such as opening a file, saving a file, and closing the current program. Next to the Office button is the **Quick Access toolbar**, which includes buttons for common Office commands.

TROUBLE

If you accidentally click the wrong command and an unwanted dialog box opens, press [Esc].

3. **Click** 🔘 **again to close it, then point to the Save button** 🔲 **on the Quick Access toolbar, but do not click it**

   You can point to any button in Office to see a description; this is a good way to learn the available choices.

4. **Click the Design tab on the Ribbon**

   To display a different tab, you click its name on the Ribbon. Each tab arranges related commands into **groups** to make features easy to find. The Themes group displays available themes in a **gallery**, or palette of choices you can browse. Many groups contain a **dialog box launcher**, an icon you can click to open a dialog box or task pane for the current group, which offers an alternative way to choose commands.

QUICK TIP

Live Preview is available in many galleries and palettes throughout Office.

5. **Move the mouse pointer** ⬚ **over the Aspect theme in the Themes group as shown in Figure A-6, but do not click the mouse button**

   Because you have not clicked the theme, you have not actually made any changes to the slide. With the **Live Preview** feature, you can point to a choice, see the results right in the document, and then decide whether you want to make the change.

QUICK TIP

If you accidentally click a theme, click the Undo button 🔄 on the Quick Access toolbar.

6. **Move** ⬚ **away from the Ribbon and towards the slide**

   If you clicked the Aspect theme, it would be applied to this slide. Instead, the slide remains unchanged.

7. **Point to the Zoom slider** 🔽 **on the status bar, then drag** 🔽 **to the right until the Zoom percentage reads 166%**

   The slide display is enlarged. Zoom tools are located on the status bar. You can drag the slider or click the plus and minus buttons to zoom in/out on an area of interest. The percentage tells you the zoom effect.

8. **Drag the Zoom slider** 🔽 **on the status bar to the left until the Zoom percentage reads 73%**

FIGURE A-5: PowerPoint program window

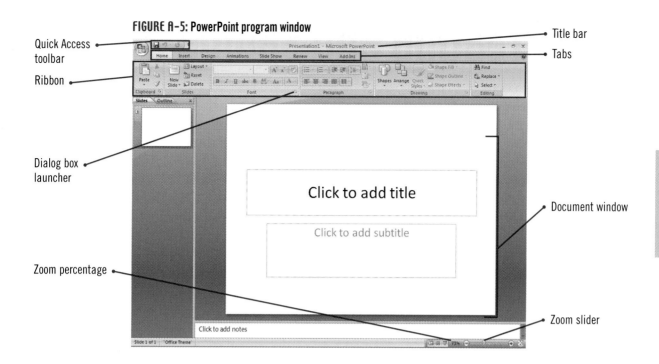

Quick Access toolbar

Ribbon

Dialog box launcher

Zoom percentage

Title bar

Tabs

Document window

Zoom slider

Office 2007

FIGURE A-6: Viewing a theme with Live Preview

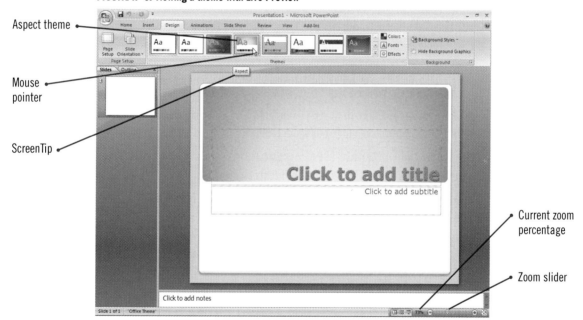

Aspect theme

Mouse pointer

ScreenTip

Current zoom percentage

Zoom slider

Customizing the Quick Access toolbar

You can customize the Quick Access toolbar to display your favorite commands. To do so, click the Customize Quick Access Toolbar button in the title bar, then click the command you want to add. If you don't see the command in the list, click More Commands to open the Customize tab of the Options dialog box. In the Options dialog box, use the Choose commands from list to choose a category, click the desired command in the list on the left, click Add to add it to the Quick Access toolbar, then click OK. To remove a button from the toolbar, click the name in the list on the right, then click Remove. To add a command to the Quick Access toolbar on the fly, simply right-click the button on the Ribbon, then click Add to Quick Access Toolbar on the shortcut menu. You can also use the Customize Quick Access Toolbar button to move the toolbar below the ribbon, by clicking Show Below the Ribbon, or to minimize the Ribbon so it takes up less space onscreen. If you click Minimize the Ribbon, the Ribbon is minimized to display only the tabs. When you click a tab, the Ribbon opens so you can choose a command; once you choose a command, the Ribbon closes again, and only the tabs are visible.

Creating and Saving a File

When working in a program, one of the first things you need to do is to create and save a file. A **file** is a stored collection of data. Saving a file enables you to work on a project now, then put it away and work on it again later. In some Office programs, including Word, Excel, and PowerPoint, a new file is automatically created when you start the program, so all you have to do is enter some data and save it. In Access, you must expressly create a file before you enter any data. You should give your files meaningful names and save them in an appropriate location, so they're easy to find. Use Microsoft Word to familiarize yourself with the process of creating and saving a document. First you'll type some notes about a possible location for a corporate meeting, then you'll save the information for later use.

STEPS

1. **Click Document1 – Microsoft Word on the taskbar**

2. **Type Locations for Corporate Meeting, then press [Enter] twice**
   The text appears in the document window, and a cursor blinks on a new blank line. The cursor indicates where the next typed text will appear.

3. **Type Las Vegas, NV, press [Enter], type Orlando, FL, press [Enter], type Chicago, IL, press [Enter] twice, then type your name**
   Compare your document to Figure A-7.

> **QUICK TIP**
> A filename can be up to 255 characters, including a file extension, and can include upper- or lowercase characters and spaces, but not ?, ", /, \, <, >, *, |, or :.

4. **Click the Save button 🖫 on the Quick Access toolbar**
   Because this is the first time you are saving this document, the Save As dialog box opens, as shown in Figure A-8. The Save As dialog box includes options for assigning a filename and storage location. Once you save a file for the first time, clicking 🖫 saves any changes to the file *without* opening the Save As dialog box, because no additional information is needed. In the Address bar, Office displays the default location for where to save the file, but you can change to any location. In the File name field, Office displays a suggested name for the document based on text in the file, but you can enter a different name.

5. **Type Potential Corporate Meeting Locations**
   The text you type replaces the highlighted text.

> **QUICK TIP**
> You can create a desktop icon that you can double-click to both launch a program and open a document, by saving it to the desktop.

6. **In the Save As dialog box, use the Address bar or Navigation pane to navigate to the drive and folder where you store your Data Files**
   Many students store files on a flash drive or Zip drive, but you can also store files on your computer, a network drive, or any storage device indicated by your instructor or technical support person.

> **QUICK TIP**
> To create a new blank file when a file is open, click the Office button, click New, then click Create.

7. **Click Save**
   The Save As dialog box closes, the new file is saved to the location you specified, then the name of the document appears in the title bar, as shown in Figure A-9. (You may or may not see a file extension.) See Table A-1 for a description of the different types of files you create in Office, and the file extensions associated with each. You can save a file in an earlier version of a program by choosing from the list of choices in the Save as type list arrow in the Save As dialog box.

TABLE A-1: Common filenames and default file extensions

File created in	is called a	and has the default extension
Excel	workbook	.xlsx
Word	document	.docx
Access	database	.accdb
PowerPoint	presentation	.pptx

FIGURE A-7: Creating a document in Word

Save button

Your name should appear here

Insertion point

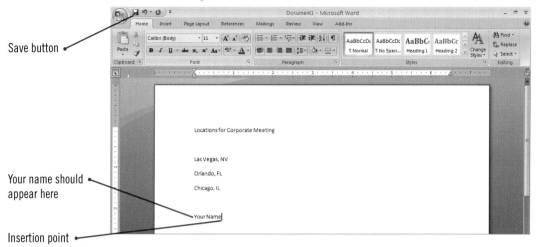

FIGURE A-8: Save As dialog box

Address bar

Navigation pane; your links and Folders setting may differ

File name field; your computer may not be set to display file extensions

Previous Locations list arrow

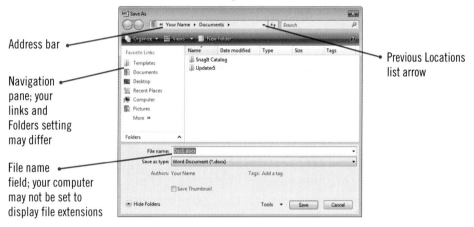

FIGURE A-9: Named Word document

Name appears in title bar

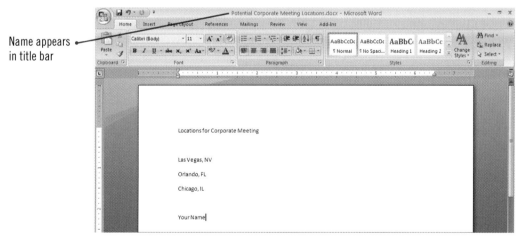

Using the Office Clipboard

You can use the Office Clipboard to cut and copy items from one Office program and paste them into others. The Clipboard can store a maximum of 24 items. To access it, open the Office Clipboard task pane by clicking the launcher in the Clipboard group in the Home tab. Each time you copy a selection, it is saved in the Office Clipboard. Each entry in the Office Clipboard includes an icon that tells you the program in which it was created. To paste an entry, click in the document where you want it to appear, then click the item in the Office Clipboard. To delete an item from the Office Clipboard, right-click the item, then click Delete.

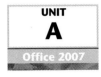

Opening a File and Saving it with a New Name

In many cases as you work in Office, you start with a blank document, but often you need to use an existing file. It might be a file you or a co-worker created earlier as a work-in-progress, or it could be a complete document that you want to use as the basis for another. For example, you might want to create a budget for this year using the budget you created last year; you could type in all the categories and information from scratch, or you could open last year's budget, save it with a new name, and just make changes to update it for the current year. By opening the existing file and saving it with the Save As command, you create a duplicate that you can modify to your heart's content, while the original file remains intact. Use Excel to open an existing workbook file, and save it with a new name so the original remains unchanged.

STEPS

QUICK TIP

If you point to a command on the Office menu that is followed by an arrow, a submenu opens displaying additional, related commands.

1. **Click Microsoft Excel – Book1 on the taskbar, click the Office button, then click Open**

   The Open dialog box opens, where you can navigate to any drive or folder location accessible to your computer to locate a file.

2. **In the Open dialog box, navigate to the drive and folder where you store your Data Files**

   The files available in the current folder are listed, as shown in Figure A-10. This folder contains one file.

3. **Click OFFICE A-1.xlsx, then click Open**

   The dialog box closes and the file opens in Excel. An Excel file is an electronic spreadsheet, so it looks different from a Word document or a PowerPoint slide.

QUICK TIP

The Recent Items list on the Office menu displays recently opened documents; you can click any file to open it.

4. **Click, then click Save As**

   The Save As dialog box opens, and the current filename is highlighted in the File name text box. Using the Save As command enables you to create a copy of the current, existing file with a new name. This action preserves the original file, and creates a new file that you can modify.

QUICK TIP

The Save As command works identically in all Office programs, except Access; in Access, this command lets you save a copy of the current database object, such as a table or form, with a new name, but not a copy of the entire database.

5. **Navigate to the drive and folder where your Data Files are stored if necessary, type Budget for Corporate Meeting in the File name text box, as shown in Figure A-11, then click Save**

   A copy of the existing document is created with the new name. The original file, Office A-1.xlsx, closes automatically.

6. **Click cell A19, type your name, then press [Enter], as shown in Figure A-12**

   In Excel, you enter data in cells, which are formed by the intersection of a row and a column. Cell A19 is at the intersection of column A and row 19. When you press [Enter], the cell pointer moves to cell A20.

7. **Click the Save button on the Quick Access toolbar**

   Your name appears in the worksheet, and your changes to the file are saved.

Exploring File Open options

You might have noticed that the Open button on the Open dialog box includes an arrow. In a dialog box, if a button includes an arrow you can click the button to invoke the command, or you can click the arrow to choose from a list of related commands. The Open button list arrow includes several related commands, including Open Read-Only and Open as Copy. Clicking Open Read-Only opens a file that you can only save by saving it with a new name; you cannot save changes to the original file. Clicking Open as Copy creates a copy of the file already saved and named with the word "Copy" in the title. Like the Save As command, these commands provide additional ways to use copies of existing files while ensuring that original files do not get inadvertently changed.

FIGURE A-10: Open dialog box

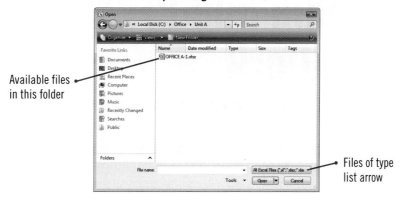

Available files
in this folder

Files of type
list arrow

FIGURE A-11: Save As dialog box

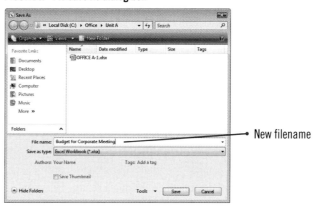

New filename

FIGURE A-12: Adding your name to the worksheet

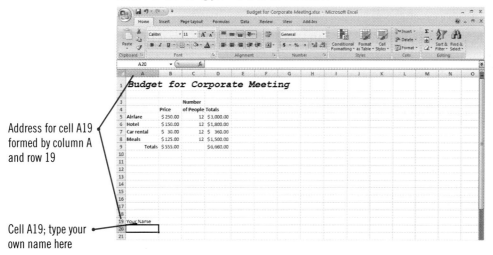

Address for cell A19
formed by column A
and row 19

Cell A19; type your
own name here

Working in Compatibility mode

Not everyone upgrades to the newest version of Office. As a general rule, new software versions are **backward-compatible**, meaning that documents saved by an older version can be read by newer software. The reverse is not always true, so Office 2007 includes a feature called Compatibility mode. When you open a file created in an earlier version of Office, "Compatibility Mode" appears in the title bar, letting you know the file was created in an earlier, but usable version of the program. If you are working with someone who may not be using the newest version of the software, you can avoid possible incompatibility problems by saving your file in

another, earlier format. To do this, click the Office button, point to the Save As command, then click a choice on the Save As submenu. For example, if you're working in Excel, click Excel 97-2003 Workbook format. When the Save As dialog box opens, you'll notice that the Save as type box reads "Excel 97-2003 Workbook" instead of the default "Excel Workbook." To see more file format choices, such as Excel 97-2003 Template or Microsoft Excel 5.0/95 Workbook, click Other Formats on the Save As submenu. In the Save As dialog box, click the Save as type button, click the choice you think matches what your co-worker is using, then click Save.

Viewing and Printing Your Work

If your computer is connected to a printer or a print server, you can easily print any Office document. Printing can be as simple as clicking a button, or as involved as customizing the print job by printing only selected pages or making other choices, and/or **previewing** the document to see exactly what a document will look like when it is printed. (In order for printing and previewing to work, a printer must be installed.) In addition to using Print Preview, each Microsoft Office program lets you switch among various **views** of the document window, to show more or fewer details or a different combination of elements that make it easier to complete certain tasks, such as formatting or reading text. You can also increase or decrease your view of a document, so you can see more or less of it on the screen at once. Changing your view of a document does not affect the file in any way, it affects only the way it looks on screen. ▰▰▰▰▰ Experiment with changing your view of a Word document, and then preview and print your work.

STEPS

1. **Click Potential Corporate Meeting Locations – Microsoft Word on the taskbar**
   Word becomes the active program, and the document fills the screen.

2. **Click the View tab on the Ribbon**
   In most Office programs, the View tab on the Ribbon includes groups and commands for changing your view of the current document. You can also change views using the View buttons on the status bar.

3. **Click Web Layout button in the Document Views group on the View tab**
   The view changes to Web Layout view, as shown in Figure A-13. This view shows how the document will look if you save it as a Web page.

   > **QUICK TIP**
   > You can also use the Zoom button in the Zoom group of the View tab to enlarge or reduce a document's appearance.

4. **Click the Zoom in button ⊕ on the status bar eight times until the zoom percentage reads 180%**
   Zooming in, or choosing a higher percentage, makes a document appear bigger on screen, but less of it fits on the screen at once; **zooming out**, or choosing a lower percentage, lets you see more of the document but at a reduced size.

5. **Drag the Zoom slider ▽ on the status bar to the center mark**
   The Zoom slider lets you zoom in and out without opening a dialog box or clicking buttons.

6. **Click the Print Layout button on the View tab**
   You return to Print Layout view, the default view in Microsoft Word.

7. **Click the Office button ⊛, point to Print, then click Print Preview**
   The Print Preview presents the most accurate view of how your document will look when printed, displaying the entire page on screen at once. Compare your screen to Figure A-14. The Ribbon in Print Preview contains a single tab, also known as a **program** tab, with commands specific to Print Preview. The commands on this tab facilitate viewing and changing overall settings such as margins and page size.

   > **QUICK TIP**
   > You can open the Print dialog box from any view by clicking the Office button, then clicking Print.

8. **Click the Print button on the Ribbon**
   The Print dialog box opens, as shown in Figure A-15. You can use this dialog box to change which pages to print, the number of printed copies, and even the number of pages you print on each page. If you have multiple printers from which to choose, you can change from one installed printer by clicking the Name list arrow, then clicking the name of the installed printer you want to use.

9. **Click OK, then click the Close Print Preview button on the Ribbon**
   A copy of the document prints, and Print Preview closes.

FIGURE A-13: Web Layout view

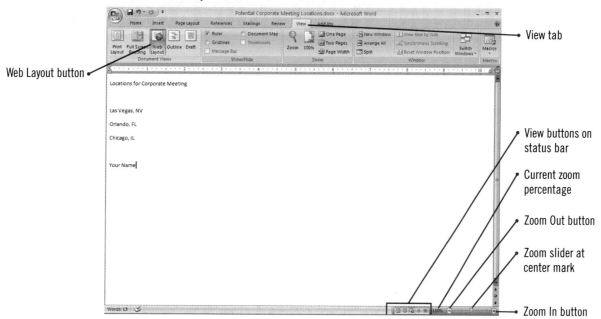

Web Layout button

View tab

View buttons on status bar

Current zoom percentage

Zoom Out button

Zoom slider at center mark

Zoom In button

FIGURE A-14: Print Preview screen

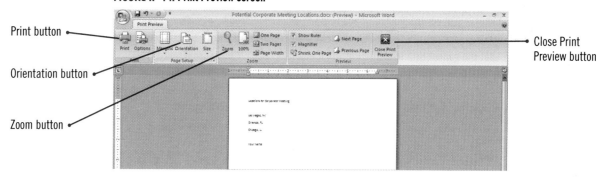

Print button

Orientation button

Zoom button

Close Print Preview button

FIGURE A-15: Print dialog box

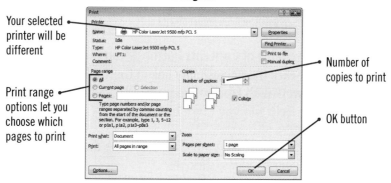

Your selected printer will be different

Print range options let you choose which pages to print

Number of copies to print

OK button

Using the Print Screen feature to create a screen capture

At some point you may want to create a screen capture. A **screen capture** is a snapshot of your screen, as if you took a picture of it with a camera. You might want to take a screen capture if an error message occurs and you want Technical Support to see exactly what's on the screen. Or perhaps your instructor wants to see what your screen looks like when you create a particular document. To create a screen capture, press [PrtScn]. (Keyboards differ, but you may find the [PrtScn] button on the Insert key in or near your keyboard's function keys. You may have to press the [F Lock] key to enable the Function keys.) Pressing this key places a digital image of your screen in the Windows temporary storage area known as the **Clipboard**. Open the document where you want the screen capture to appear, click the Home tab on the Ribbon (if necessary), then click Paste on the Home tab. The screen capture is pasted into the document.

Getting Help and Closing a File

You can get comprehensive help at any time by pressing [F1] in an Office program. You can also get help in the form of a ScreenTip by pointing to almost any icon in the program window. When you're finished working in an Office document, you have a few choices regarding ending your work session. You can close a file or exit a program by using the Office button or by clicking a button on the title bar. Closing a file leaves a program running, while exiting a program closes all the open files in that program as well as the program itself. In all cases, Office reminds you if you try to close a file or exit a program and your document contains unsaved changes. ░░░░ Explore the Help system in Microsoft Office, and then close your documents and exit any open programs.

STEPS

1. **Point to the Zoom button on the View tab of the Ribbon**
   A ScreenTip appears that describes how the Zoom button works.

> **QUICK TIP**
> If you are not connected to the Internet, the Help window displays only the help content available on your computer.

2. **Press [F1]**
   The Word Help window opens, as shown in Figure A-16, displaying the home page for help in Word. Each entry is a hyperlink you can click to open a list of related topics. This window also includes a toolbar of useful Help commands and a Search field. The connection status at the bottom of the Help window indicates that the connection to Office Online is active. Office Online supplements the help content available on your computer with a wide variety of up-to-date topics, templates, and training.

3. **Click the Getting help link in the Table of Contents pane**
   The icon next to Getting help changes and its list of subtopics expands.

> **QUICK TIP**
> You can also open the Help window by clicking the Microsoft Office Help button 🔘 to the right of the tabs on the Ribbon.

4. **Click the Work with the Help window link in the topics list in the left pane**
   The topic opens in the right pane, as shown in Figure A-17.

5. **Click the Hide Table of Contents button 🔲 on the Help toolbar**
   The left pane closes, as shown in Figure A-18.

> **QUICK TIP**
> You can print the current topic by clicking the Print button 🖨 on the Help toolbar to open the Print dialog box.

6. **Click the Show Table of Contents button 🔖 on the Help toolbar, scroll to the bottom of the left pane, click the Accessibility link in the Table of Contents pane, click the Use the keyboard to work with Ribbon programs link, read the information in the right pane, then click the Help window Close button**

7. **Click the Office button 🔘, then click Close; if a dialog box opens asking whether you want to save your changes, click Yes**
   The Potential Corporate Meeting Locations document closes, leaving the Word program open.

8. **Click 🔘, then click Exit Word**
   Microsoft Office Word closes, and the Excel program window is active.

9. **Click 🔘, click Exit Excel, click the PowerPoint button on the taskbar if necessary, click 🔘, then click Exit PowerPoint**
   Microsoft Office Excel and Microsoft Office PowerPoint both close.

FIGURE A-16: Word Help window

Help toolbar

Search field

Hide Table of
Contents
button

The colors
of your links
may differ

Connection status

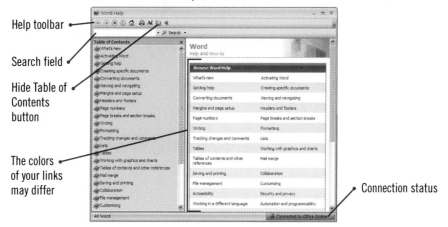

FIGURE A-17: Work with the Help window

Print button

Icon indicates
expanded topic

Work with
the Help
window link

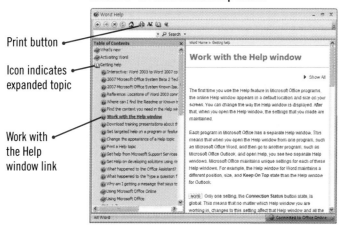

FIGURE A-18: Help window with Table of Contents closed

Show Table of
Contents button

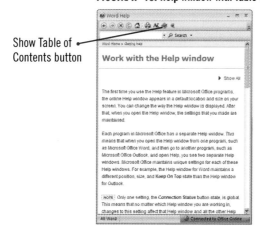

Recovering a document

Sometimes while you are using Office, you may experience a power failure or your computer may "freeze," making it impossible to continue working. If this type of interruption occurs, each Office program has a built-in recovery feature that allows you to open and save files that were open at the time of the interruption. When you restart the program(s) after an interruption, the Document Recovery task pane opens on the left side of your screen displaying both original and recovered versions of the files that were open. If you're not

sure which file to open (original or recovered), it's usually better to open the recovered file because it will contain the latest information. You can, however, open and review all versions of the file that were recovered and save the best one. Each file listed in the Document Recovery task pane displays a list arrow with options that allow you to open the file, save it as is, delete it, or show repairs made to it during recovery.

Office 2007

Practice

If you have a SAM user profile, you may have access to hands-on instruction, practice, and assessment of the skills covered in this unit. Log in to your SAM account (http://sam2007.course.com/) to launch any assigned training activities or exams that relate to the skills covered in this unit.

▼ CONCEPTS REVIEW

Label the elements of the program window shown in Figure A-19.

FIGURE A-19

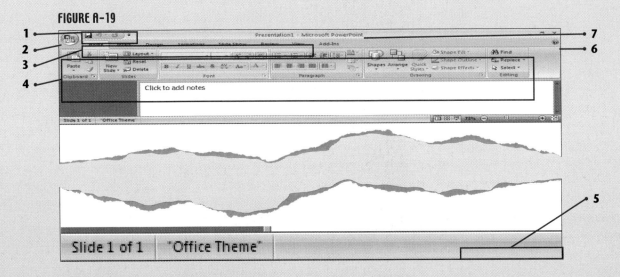

Match each project with the program for which it is best suited.

8. Microsoft Office PowerPoint   **a.** Corporate expansion budget with expense projections

9. Microsoft Office Excel   **b.** Business résumé for a job application

10. Microsoft Office Word   **c.** Auto parts store inventory

11. Microsoft Office Access   **d.** Presentation for Board of Directors meeting

▼ INDEPENDENT CHALLENGE 1

You just accepted an administrative position with a local car dealership that's recently invested in computers and is now considering purchasing Microsoft Office. You are asked to propose ways Office might help the dealership. You produce your proposal in Microsoft Word.

a. Start Word, then save the document as **Microsoft Office Proposal** in the drive and folder where you store your Data Files.

b. Type **Microsoft Office Word**, press [Enter] twice, type **Microsoft Office Excel**, press [Enter] twice, type **Microsoft Office PowerPoint**, press [Enter] twice, type **Microsoft Office Access**, press [Enter] twice, then type your name.

c. Click the line beneath each program name, type at least two tasks suited to that program, then press [Enter].

d. Save your work, then print one copy of this document.

Advanced Challenge Exercise

- Press the [PrtScn] button to create a screen capture, then press [Ctrl][V].
- Save and print the document.

e. Exit Word.

Upgrading to Word 2007

For users of previous versions of Microsoft Word, Word 2007 can look a bit intimidating. The new look of the program, fresh techniques for accomplishing once-familiar tasks, and rich offering of innovative features, all present a different way of interacting with your word processing program. But once you get familiar with the new Word, you'll be creating great-looking documents more quickly than ever. In this unit, you will learn what's changed—and what hasn't—in Word 2007, and get hands-on practice using the program.

OBJECTIVES

Word 2007 Overview: What's New?

Learn new ways to perform tasks

Learn new editing and formatting techniques

Learn new page formatting techniques

Learn new ways to work with graphics

Learn to use building blocks

Learn new ways to add references

Learn new ways to review documents

Learn new ways to distribute documents

Word 2007 Overview: What's New?

Compared to earlier versions of Microsoft Word, Word 2007 includes more sophisticated editing and formatting features, greater flexibility with graphics, and easier ways to finalize, proof, and share documents. 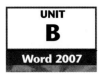 In this lesson, take a quick tour of the most important changes in Word 2007.

DETAILS

As you start using Word 2007, you will find changes in the following major program areas:

- **New ways to perform program tasks**

  One of the most exciting changes in Word 2007 is the user interface, as shown in Figure B-1. From tabs on the Ribbon to the buttons on the status bar, each element in the program window brings commands and options into easier reach, so you spend less time clicking to find the one you want. Some methods will be familiar to previous users of Word. You'll find shortcut menus for many tasks, available when you right-click a selection. You'll also find that you can use most keyboard commands from Word 2003.

- **New ways to edit and format**

  In Word 2003, you edited and formatted text using the Edit and Format menus. While basic editing has not changed significantly in Word 2007, your formatting options have. Familiar features such as templates and styles have been upgraded and new features have been added, many of which let you apply multiple formatting changes at once. New and improved features include Quick Styles for making paragraph and text changes, themes for making document-wide changes, table styles, picture styles, and margin presets. Figure B-2 shows a document created using a Word 2007 template, with a theme applied.

- **New ways to insert and work with graphics**

  In Word 2003, you inserted graphics, tables, and special elements such as WordArt using the Insert menu. With Word 2007, you can insert these types of objects and many more using the Insert tab on the Ribbon. In addition to a wider variety of tables, pictures, Clip Art, shapes, and WordArt, you can add SmartArt graphics, a collection of diagrams that are easy to customize with your own text.

- **New ways to reuse content**

  In Word 2003, AutoText was a useful tool for reusing signature lines and other repetitive text in a document. In Word 2007, AutoText is just one gallery within Quick Parts, a feature that lets you add all types of preformatted content to documents. Each Word template includes a selection of cover pages, headers and footers, and other preformatted Quick Parts, and you can create your own building blocks from any text—even a table—and make it available as part of this feature. Using the Building Blocks Organizer, shown in Figure B-3, you can edit and manage your own building blocks, as well as those provided with Word 2007.

- **Other new features**

  New and improved reference features take the guesswork out of creating footnotes, cross-references, citations, and bibliographies. Spelling and Grammar features also have been expanded considerably. Programs across the Office suite can share a custom dictionary, as well as many global settings, such as ignoring Internet and file addresses. Like Word 2003, Word 2007 includes a Research pane for searching multiple online sources such as the Encarta Dictionary or Encyclopedia. But the new Research pane incorporates many more sources, including business and financial sites.

  The new XML-based file format for Word documents makes for smaller file sizes and easier document recovery. You can also save a document in more than 20 other formats. If you install an add-in available from Microsoft, you can also save a document directly to PDF or XPS. Bloggers can publish a document as a new post, and co-workers can publish to a document management server.

FIGURE B-1: Word 2003 and Word 2007 program windows

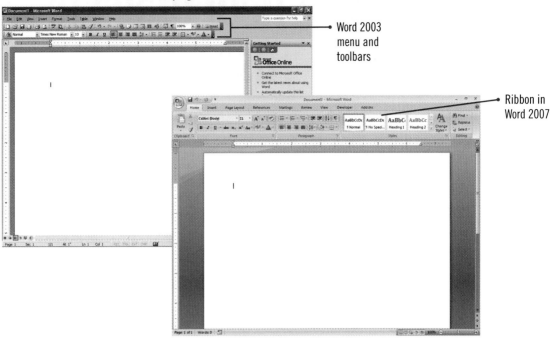

Word 2003 menu and toolbars

Ribbon in Word 2007

FIGURE B-2: Document created in Word 2007

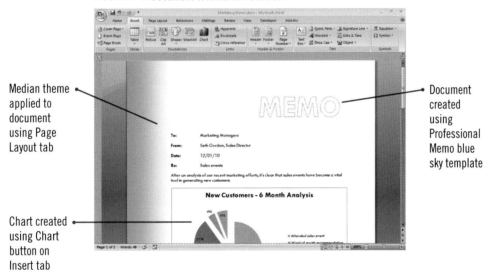

Median theme applied to document using Page Layout tab

Document created using Professional Memo blue sky template

Chart created using Chart button on Insert tab

FIGURE B-3: Building Blocks Organizer

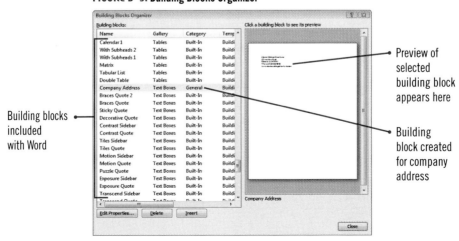

Preview of selected building block appears here

Building block created for company address

Building blocks included with Word

Learning New Ways to Perform Tasks

To take advantage of the new features in Word 2007, you'll want to be familiar with the new way to access commands and navigate a document. Most commands are easy to find because they are organized into groups and tabs that clearly identify their purpose, such as Insert or Mailings. Note that there is no File tab or Edit tab in Word 2007; instead, you use the Office button menu to save and open documents, and the Home tab to perform basic editing commands. In this lesson, examine the new Word program window and start working with a document.

STEPS

1. **Start Microsoft Word 2007**

   Word starts, a blank document opens, and the Home tab of the Ribbon appears in front of the other tabs. The Home tab includes commands for common editing and formatting tasks. See Table B-1 for a description of the tabs that appear by default on the Ribbon and the types of commands they contain.

2. **Click the Office button 🔵, click Open, navigate to the drive and folder where you store your Data Files, open the file B-1.docx, then save it as Classic Walking Adventures**

   The Office menu contains many commands formerly found on the File menu in Word 2003, such as Open, Close, and Save As, as well as a recent documents list. The Office menu also contains the Word Options button, which you can use to set program options, such as changing your user information.

3. **Click the table**

   The table is selected for editing, and two Table Tools contextual tabs appear on the Ribbon: Table Tools Design and Table Tools Layout.

4. **Click the Table Tools Design tab, if necessary, click the More button ▼ in the Table Styles group, click the Colorful List—Accent 2 style (second column, fifth row under Built-In), then compare your screen to Figure B-4**

   You used a built-in Table Style to format the table.

5. **Click anywhere in the heading, Summer at Last!**

   The Table Tools Design tab closes, and the Home tab opens. This text is formatted in bold, so the Bold button in the Font group on the Ribbon is highlighted.

6. **Right-click the Bold button 🅱 in the Font group, then click Add to Quick Access Toolbar**

   The Bold button is added to the Quick Access toolbar. By default, the Quick Access toolbar in Word contains three buttons: Save, Undo, and Redo. You can add almost any command to this toolbar by right-clicking it on the Ribbon and then clicking Add to Quick Access Toolbar.

7. **Right-click 🅱 on the Quick Access toolbar, then click Remove from Quick Access Toolbar**

   If you are working in a classroom or office environment where other people share a computer, it's best not to customize the program window.

8. **Click the Page: 1 of 2 button on the status bar**

   The Go To tab of the Find and Replace dialog box opens, as shown in Figure B-5. Some controls on the status bar not only display information, but also open useful dialog boxes. The **Proofing errors button** on the status bar informs you that proofing errors were found in this document. You will correct these errors in a future lesson.

9. **Type 2, click Go To, click Close, then click the Save button 💾 on the Quick Access Toolbar**

   The insertion point moves to the top of Page 2, and your changes are saved to the document.

FIGURE B-4: Applying a Table Style

Currently selected style appears at the top of the gallery

Table Tools Design tab

More button

Colorful List— Accent 2 Table style applied to table

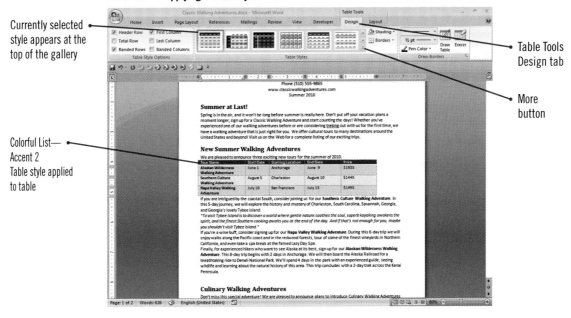

FIGURE B-5: Using the Go To feature

Go To tab

Page: 1 of 2 button

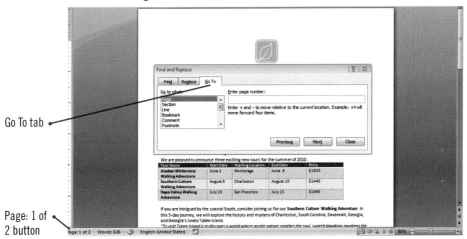

TABLE B-1: Ribbon tabs in Word

tab	contains these groups	Office 2003 menu locations
Home	Clipboard, Font, Paragraph, Styles, Editing	File menu, Edit menu
Insert	Pages, Table, Illustrations, Links, Header & Footer, Text, Symbols	Insert menu
Page Layout	Themes, Page Setup, Page Background, Paragraph, Arrange	Format menu
References	Table of Contents, Footnotes, Citations & Bibliography, Captions, Index, Table of Authorities	Insert menu
Mailings	Create, Start Mail Merge, Write & Insert Fields, Preview Results, Finish	Tools menu
Review	Proofing, Comments, Tracking, Changes, Compare, Protect	Tools menu
View	Document Views, Show/Hide, Zoom, Window, Macros	View menu
Developer	Code, Controls, XML, Protect, Templates	Tools menu
Add-Ins	Custom Toolbars	Add-Ins menu

Learning New Editing and Formatting Techniques

The Home tab on the Ribbon includes buttons for many editing and formatting tasks that are familiar to Word 2003 users, such as Copy, Bold, and Italic. But you'll also find additional buttons, including Change Case, Grow Font, Shrink Font, and Line Spacing. Dialog boxes are still available for most tasks, but with so many buttons available on the Ribbon and Mini toolbar, you don't need to use them as often. The Live Preview feature, available in many style galleries, lets you see how a change will look before you actually make a selection. The Styles group on the Home tab offers a new way to apply and work with styles. You can preview and apply styles using the Quick Styles gallery in this group. You can use the Change Styles button to change the overall look, colors, or fonts of all styles in a document with a single click. In this lesson, practice using new editing and formatting techniques.

STEPS

1. **In the first line under the heading** Culinary Walking Adventures, **select the entire sentence,** Don't miss this special adventure!

   ### QUICK TIP
   To use the Paste Special dialog box when pasting a selection, click the Paste button arrow in the Clipboard group, then click Paste Special.

2. **Click the** Cut button ✄ **in the Clipboard group on the Home tab, click the end of the paragraph after the sentence that ends** local chefs., **press [Spacebar], then click the** Paste button **in the Clipboard group**

   The selection is pasted at the end of the paragraph, as shown in Figure B-6. As in Word 2003, the Paste Options button appears so that you can specify how to format the pasted selection if you wish.

3. **Move to** page 1, **then select the text that begins** "To visit **and ends** visit Tybee Island."; **make sure to select the quotation marks**

   This text is formatted in the Normal style, in 11-point Calibri, the Word 2007 default font and font size.

   ### QUICK TIP
   To apply a paragraph style, simply click in the paragraph you want to format before applying the style.

4. **Click the** More button ▾ **in the Styles group on the Home tab**

   The Styles gallery opens, as shown in Figure B-7, displaying popular styles you can apply to paragraphs or selected text. Clicking the dialog box launcher in this group displays a complete list of available styles, including a New Style button 📝 for creating a new style, a Style Inspector button 🔍 to check the formatting of any text, and a Manage Styles button 📝 that opens the Manage Styles dialog box.

5. **Point to various styles in the gallery, observe the live preview in your document, then click the** Quote style **(third column, third row)**

   ### QUICK TIP
   To change the colors used in the styles within your document, point to Colors in the Change Styles list and then. Click a different Colors set; to change the fonts used, point to Fonts and then choose a different Fonts set.

6. **Click the** Change Styles button **in the Styles group, point to** Style Set, **then click** Modern

   All styles in the document change to the Modern Style Set. A **Quick Style Set** is a group of coordinated styles that work well together. Some styles have already been applied to this document; for example, the Heading 1 style has been applied to all the paragraph headings. These headings are highlighted in blue because the Modern Quick Style Set includes colored backgrounds for the Heading 1 style.

7. **Select the first line in the document,** Classic Walking Adventures News

   The Mini toolbar fades in near the selected text, as shown in Figure B-8.

8. **Click the** Font Size list arrow **on the Mini toolbar, then click** 24

9. **Click away from the selected text, then click the** Save button 💾 **on the Quick Access Toolbar**

FIGURE B-6: Cutting and pasting a selection

Paste button

Cut button

Selection is pasted here and Paste Options button appears

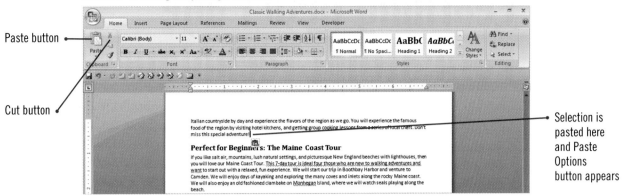

FIGURE B-7: Cutting and pasting a selection

Selected text

Currently selected style

Quote style

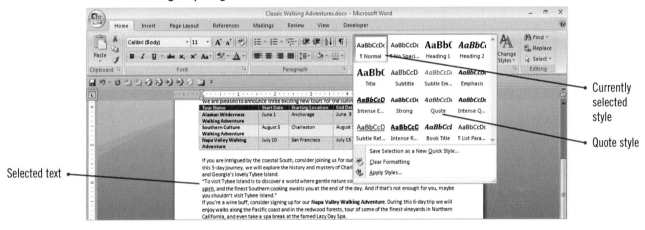

FIGURE B-8: Formatting a selection using the Mini toolbar

Selected text

Mini toolbar

Font Size list arrow

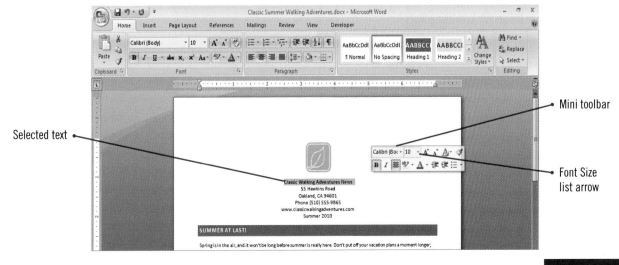

Learning New Page Formatting Techniques

When you need to make overall changes to a document, you'll appreciate the new page formatting features in Word 2007. Many of these features are available on the Page Layout tab. You can use this tab to apply and modify themes, add page backgrounds, and change margins, tabs and indents without opening a dialog box or hunting through menus. A **theme** is a coordinated set of formatting elements, including colors. Themes were available in Word 2003, but in Word 2007 it's easier to apply and customize themes with different sets of colors, fonts, and effects. ▓▓▓▓▓ In this lesson, practice using the new page formatting features in Word by changing the look of the Classic Walking Adventures document.

STEPS

1. **Click the** Page Layout tab **on the Ribbon**

2. **Click the** Page Color button **in the Page Background group, point to the** Tan, Background 2 **color (third column, first row under Theme Colors), as shown in Figure B-9, then click the color**

3. **Click the** Themes button **in the Themes group**
   The Themes gallery opens, as shown in Figure B-10. The current theme, Office, is highlighted in yellow.

4. **Point to various themes, preview the changes in the document, then click** Oriel
   The Oriel theme is applied to the document. When you apply a theme, the colors, fonts, and visual effects change to the new theme. The background color changes to yellow because this is the Background 2 shade in the Oriel theme. Colors, fonts, and effects are designed to be used together, but you can mix and match colors, fonts, and effects from other themes to achieve the mix you want.

5. **Click the** Theme Colors button ▦ **in the Themes group, then click** Paper
   Paper theme colors are applied to the document. See Figure B-11.

6. **Click the** Margins button **in the Page Setup group**
   A list of margin presets opens. You can click any choice to change all margin settings for the document at once, or click Custom Margins to open the Margins tab of the Page Setup dialog box.

7. **Click** Office 2003 Default **in the Margins list, as shown in Figure B-12**
   Word 2007 includes several preset formats for users who want quick access to default settings from the previous version of Word. See Table B-2 for an overview of how the default template has changed.

8. **Click the** Margins button, **click** Normal, **then save your changes to the document**

TABLE B-2: Changes to the default template in Word

setting	Word 2003 default setting	Word 2007 default setting
Normal default font	Times New Roman 12 pt	Calibri 11 pt
Line spacing	1.0 (single)	1.15
Top margin	1	1"
Left Margin	1.25"	1"
Right Margin	1.25"	1"
Bottom Margin	1"	1"
Line spacing after a paragraph	Next line down	Second line down
Color scheme	Black and white	Black, white, blue, and other colors based on Office theme

Upgrading to Word 2007

FIGURE B-9: Applying a background color

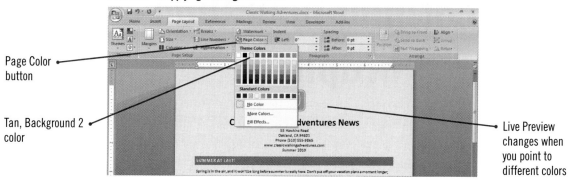

Page Color button

Tan, Background 2 color

Live Preview changes when you point to different colors

FIGURE B-10: Themes gallery

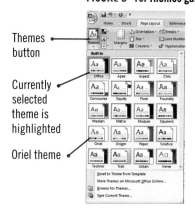

Themes button

Currently selected theme is highlighted

Oriel theme

FIGURE B-11: New color theme applied to document

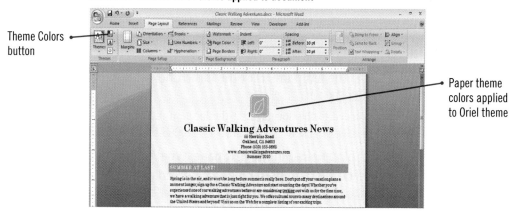

Theme Colors button

Paper theme colors applied to Oriel theme

FIGURE B-12: Changing the margins

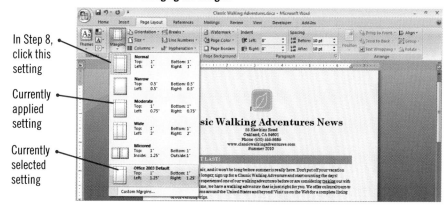

In Step 8, click this setting

Currently applied setting

Currently selected setting

Learning New Ways to Work with Graphics

Modifying a graphic object is much easier than it was in Word 2003, thanks to more robust capabilities in Word 2007. The Insert tab includes buttons for inserting and drawing almost any object you can imagine, including tables, Clip Art, three-dimensional shapes, charts, WordArt, and a new feature called SmartArt. **SmartArt graphics** are professionally designed diagrams, such as organization charts and process diagrams, that you can insert and customize. Galleries such as Picture Styles, Table Styles, and SmartArt Styles make it easy to change the look of a graphic with a single click. New formatting options include transparency and drop shadow effects. ▓▓▓▓▓ In this lesson, practice working with graphics by modifying an existing graphic and adding a SmartArt diagram to the Classic Walking Adventures document.

STEPS

QUICK TIP

The Recolor gallery displays colors that vary based on the currently applied theme.

QUICK TIP

To insert WordArt in a document, click the WordArt button in the Text group on the Insert tab; to convert existing text to WordArt, select the text, then click the WordArt button.

TROUBLE

If the SmartArt diagram text pane does not open automatically, click the Text pane controls on the left edge of the SmartArt pane.

1. **Double-click the picture of the leaf at the top of the document**

   The object is selected, and the Picture Tools Format tab opens, containing tools for formatting and modifying the selected picture.

2. **Click the Recolor button in the Adjust group, point to the Accent color 1 Dark color style (second column under Dark Variations) as shown in Figure B-13, then click the style**

3. **Scroll to page 2, click at the beginning of the first sentence which starts Finally, for experienced hikers, then click the Insert tab**

   The Insert tab opens, with groups of commands for inserting tables, illustrations, and other elements.

4. **Click the SmartArt button in the Illustrations group**

   The Choose a SmartArt Graphic dialog box opens. To choose a SmartArt graphic, you first choose the type of graphic you want, such as List or Process, in the category list in the left pane. Each category contains several layouts, which appear in the middle pane. When you click a layout, a preview of the design and guidelines for when and how to use it appear in the right pane.

5. **Click Process in the left pane, click the Basic Chevron Process layout (first column, third row), then click OK**

   The diagram is added to the document at the location of the insertion point, and a text pane opens for entering your text. See Figure B-15. You can type in either the text pane or the diagram.

6. **Click first text placeholder in the text pane, type Anchorage, click the second placeholder, type Denali, click the third placeholder, type Kenai, then click the Close button ☒ on the text pane**

7. **Click the Smart Art Tools Format tab, click the Size button, type 1 in the Height box, type 3 in the Width box, press [Enter], click the Arrange button, click Text Wrapping, then click Tight**

8. **Click the SmartArt Tools Design tab, click the Moderate Effect style in the SmartArt Styles group, click away from the diagram, then save your changes**

   The diagram is formatted with a dark green gradient fill color and subtle drop-shadow effect, as shown in Figure B-15.

FIGURE B-13: Recoloring a picture

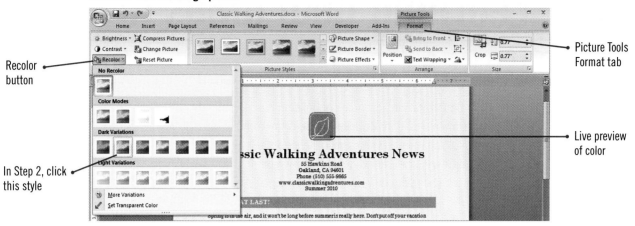

Recolor button

In Step 2, click this style

Picture Tools Format tab

Live preview of color

FIGURE B-14: Customizing a SmartArt graphic

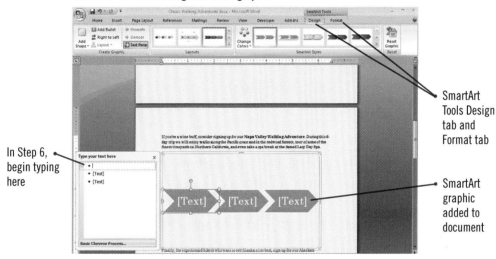

In Step 6, begin typing here

SmartArt Tools Design tab and Format tab

SmartArt graphic added to document

FIGURE B-15: Completed SmartArt diagram

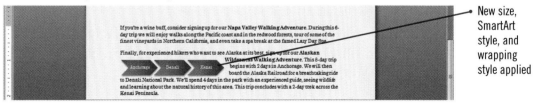

New size, SmartArt style, and wrapping style applied

Inserting graphics

Adding different types of graphics to a document is easy using commands in the Illustrations group on the Insert tab. To add a picture, click the Picture button in the Illustrations group; the Insert Picture dialog box opens, just as in Word 2003. Similarly, to insert a clip art object, click the Clip Art button, and the familiar Clip Art task pane opens. Word 2007 offers a wide variety of pictures, photos, movies, and sounds, with additional files available through Office Online. Clicking the Shapes button in the Illustrations group opens a large palette of shapes (many more than were available on the Drawing toolbar in Word 2003) as well as a Drawing Canvas for creating your own drawings. To insert a chart, click the Chart button, then use the Insert Chart dialog box to choose from a wide variety of chart types, including 3D styles. An Excel worksheet opens with placeholder data for the chart type you choose; after you replace the data with your own labels and values, close the worksheet. Excel closes, and the chart in your Word document is updated with the data you entered.

Learning New Ways to Reuse Content

You can save time by taking advantage of building blocks, content controls, and other features designed to speed up document creation. **Building blocks** are formatted text or graphic selections you can insert in any document. Word comes with many galleries of built-in building blocks, such as Headers, Footers, Page Numbers, and Cover Pages. You can add your own entries or add a building block to the Quick Parts gallery on the Insert tab. Content controls are structured placeholders that allow a user to enter specific types of information, such as text or a picture, or to choose from a predefined set of choices. Many building blocks include content controls, which you can add to forms, templates, and other documents. Practice using content by working with building blocks features.

STEPS

1. **Click the Insert tab on the Ribbon, then click the Footer button in the Header & Footer group**

   The Footer gallery opens, displaying several built-in footer designs. Word includes several coordinated sets of theme-specific designs for building blocks, including Alphabet, Contrast, and Motion.

2. **Click the Alphabet footer**

   A new footer based on the Alphabet design is added to the document, and the Header & Footer Tools Design tab appears, as shown in Figure B-16. This tab includes commands for customizing the footer, designating on which pages you want it to appear, and navigating through the document. The Alphabet footer contains one control for adding any type of text and page number information.

3. **Click the Type text control in the footer, type Filename:, press [Spacebar], click the Quick Parts button on the Insert tab, then click Field**

   The Field dialog box opens, containing more than 60 fields you can insert.

4. **Scroll in the Field names list, click FileName, then click OK**

5. **Click the Close Header and Footer button in the Close group, click the Insert tab on the Ribbon, click the Cover Page button in the Pages group, then click the Alphabet cover page (first column, first row)**

   A new cover page based on the Alphabet design is added to the document. The cover page includes content controls for a title, subtitle, date, and author name.

6. **Click [Type the document title], type Summer Tours, click the [Type the document subtitle], type Classic Walking Adventures, click [Pick the Date], navigate to and click today's date, then type your name, if necessary**

   See Figure B-17. Depending on your Office settings, your name may already appear in the Author content control. Word customizes content controls and other placeholders with your personalized information, where available.

7. **Move to page 2, select the address and phone number in lines 2 through 4, click the Text Box button in the Text group, then click Save Selection to Text Box gallery**

   The Create New Building Block dialog box opens, as shown in Figure B-18. You can enter a name for the building block, such as Company Address, or a description.

8. **Click the Gallery list arrow, read the list of options, then click the list arrow again**

   You can specify in which gallery this building block should be available.

9. **Click Cancel, then save your changes to the document**

FIGURE B-16: Adding a built-in footer

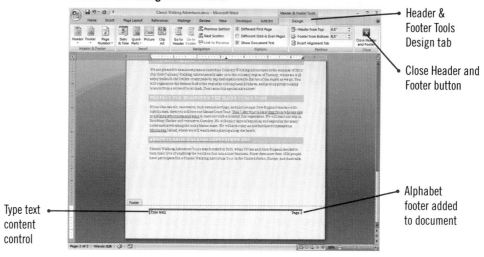

Header & Footer Tools Design tab

Close Header and Footer button

Alphabet footer added to document

Type text content control

FIGURE B-17: Customizing a built-in cover page

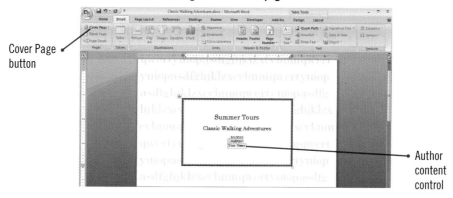

Cover Page button

Author content control

FIGURE B-18: Create New Building Block dialog box

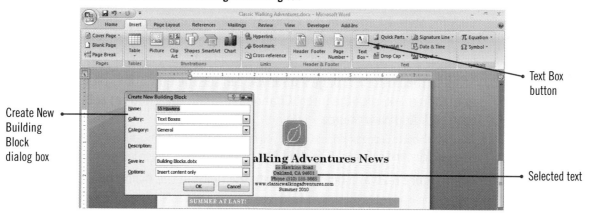

Text Box button

Create New Building Block dialog box

Selected text

Working with templates

Word 2007 includes a wider variety of templates than Word 2003, many with placeholders and other elements that help you complete the document. To create a new document from a template, click the Office button, then click New to open the New Document dialog box. The left pane of this dialog box lists categories of templates installed on your computer or available on Office online, the middle pane displays the templates in the currently selected category, and the right pane displays a preview of the currently selected template.

Word also makes it easier to save documents as templates. To save a copy of the current document as a template, click the Office button, point to Save As, then click Word Template. You can also use any existing document as a template. In the New dialog box, click New from existing in the left pane; navigate to the document you want to use, click Create, and a new document based on the existing document opens in the document window.

Learning New Ways to Add References

Papers, scholarly articles, and other formal documents may require that you cite your sources and provide footnotes or endnotes. The new and improved reference features in Word make this task much easier. Adding and updating a table of contents or index for a long document is quicker, with simplified commands and formatting choices available on the Ribbon. The new bibliography feature makes it easier to both manage and display your sources. First, you use the Insert Citation button on the References tab to record all the sources for a document. Word guides you through entering citation data by displaying a dialog box customized for the publishing style you choose. Once you've entered a source, you can use it again later without retyping all the information, even if you need to switch to a different publishing style. When you're ready, you can then use the Insert Bibliography command to insert a list of all your sources. ▰▰▰ In this lesson, practice adding references to the Classic Walking Adventures document.

STEPS

QUICK TIP

To add a caption that appears below a picture, select the picture, click the Insert Caption button in the Captions group on the References tab, then use the Caption dialog box to specify a caption and where it should appear.

1. **Scroll down to the paragraph under CULINARY WALKING ADVENTURES, click the end of the sentence that ends special adventure!, then click the References tab on the Ribbon**
   The References tab includes groups for adding a variety of references to a document.

2. **Click the Insert Footnote button in the Footnotes group**
   A footnote reference is added and the insertion point moves to the bottom of the page just above the footer so you can type the footnote text.

3. **Type This tour requires that you have a valid passport., as shown in Figure B-19**

4. **Point to the footnote reference in the paragraph, then read the ScreenTip**
   When you add footnotes and endnotes in Word 2007, the text of the note is added to a ScreenTip that appears when you point to the reference.

QUICK TIP

The Modern Language Association (MLA) style manual is used often in academia for research papers in the humanities, while the American Psychological Association (APA) style manual is used more in social sciences.

5. **Click the Style list arrow in the Citations & Bibliography group, then click MLA, if necessary**
   The first step in adding a citation to a document is to specify the publishing style for your intended bibliography. You can choose from one of ten standard publishing guidelines, including MLA and APA.

6. **Scroll to the bottom of page 2 until you can see the quotation, click after the closing quotation mark, click the Insert Citation button in the Citations & Bibliography group, then click Add New Source**
   The Create Source dialog box opens where you can enter relevant information about the source such as author, title, year, city, and publisher. The default Type of Source is book, which is appropriate for this quotation.

7. **Using Figure B-20 as a guide, complete the fields in the dialog box, then click OK**
   The citation is added to the sources for this document, and a source reference is added to the quotation.

8. **Scroll to the end of the document, click at the end of the last paragraph, click the Bibliography button in the Citations & Bibliography group, then click Works Cited**
   A bibliography based on the Word Cited style is added at the location of the insertion point, as shown in Figure B-21.

9. **If the bibliography forces the footnote to wrap to the next page, delete the blank line above the footnote, then save your changes to the document**

FIGURE B-19: Adding a footnote

References tab

Insert Footnote button

Footnote text

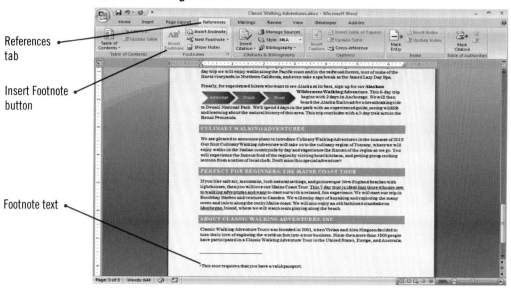

FIGURE B-20: Adding a citation source

Insert Citation button

In Step 6, click here to add citation

Completed dialog box

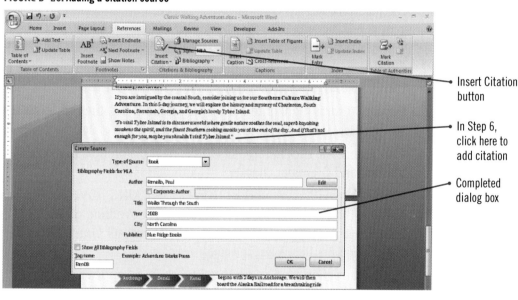

FIGURE B-21: Bibliography added to document

Learning New Ways to Review Documents

The Review tab on the Ribbon pulls together tools that were once found on the Tools, Insert, and View menus of Word 2003. You'll find proofing, commenting, tracking, comparing, and protection commands all in this central location. In addition, you'll see more options for how to use these tools, and new features such as a translation ScreenTip. Changes to the spelling and grammar features allow you to set preferences or add words to a custom dictionary in one Office program, and your changes are applied throughout the Office suite. In addition to a full set of tracking and reviewing features, new options for comparing and combining documents give you greater control over your final document. ░▒▓ Get familiar with the new proofing tools by checking spelling and grammar in the Classic Walking Adventures document, and making some final wording changes.

STEPS

1. **Click the Review tab on the Ribbon, then click the Spelling & Grammar button in the Proofing group**

   The Spelling and Grammar dialog box opens. This dialog box looks similar to the one in Word 2003, as shown in Figure B-22. However, if you add a word to the dictionary or change other options, such as ignoring words in all uppercase, your changes are applied to the other Office programs as well. The first word flagged is *treking*.

2. **Click Verify that trekking is highlighted in the Suggestions list, then click Change**

   The next word flagged is *four*. The new homonym checker in Word has spotted this as a possible word choice error.

3. **Verify that for is highlighted in the Suggestions list, then click Change**

   The next flagged word, Monhegan, is spelled correctly in this context.

4. **Click Ignore All, click Ignore Rule in the next dialog box, then click OK to close the Spelling and Grammar checker**

QUICK TIP
Word includes tools for translating text into 14 languages.

5. **Scroll to the paragraph under CULINARY WALKING ADVENTURES, select the word Tuscany, then click the Translate button in the Proofing group**

   The Research pane opens, as shown in Figure B-23, with the Translation selected. In this pane, you can access dictionaries, thesauruses, and other reference tools.

QUICK TIP
You can use the Translation ScreenTip to display an instant translation of any word you point to in a document; to use it click the Translation ScreenTip button 📖 in the Proofing group, then choose from one of four languages.

6. **In the Translation area, verify that English (U.S.) appears in the From field, click the To arrow, click Italian (Italy), then click the Start searching button ➡ next to the word Tuscany at the top of the pane**

   A translation of the word, *Toscana*, appears under the Online Bilingual Dictionary.

7. **In the document, replace the word Tuscany with Toscana, double-click Toscana, then click the Italic button 𝐼 on the Mini toolbar**

8. **Select the word famous in the next sentence, then click the Thesaurus button in the Proofing group**

   The Research pane displays Thesaurus tools and suggests alternatives to this word.

9. **Point to legendary in the list of words, click the list arrow that appears as shown in Figure B-24, click Insert, then save your changes to the document**

FIGURE B-22: Spelling and Grammar dialog box

In Windows XP, this dialog box is titled Spelling and Grammar: English (U.S.)

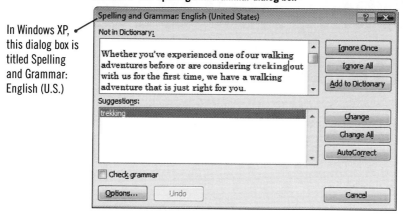

FIGURE B-23: Research pane

Translate button

Selected word

Start searching button

To list arrow

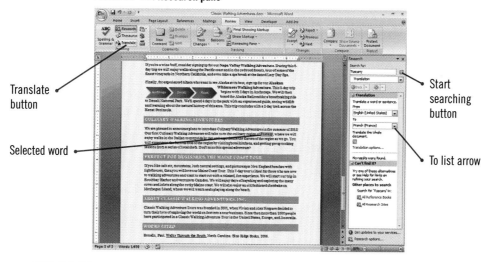

FIGURE B-24: Using the Thesaurus feature

Selected text

List arrow appears when you point to word

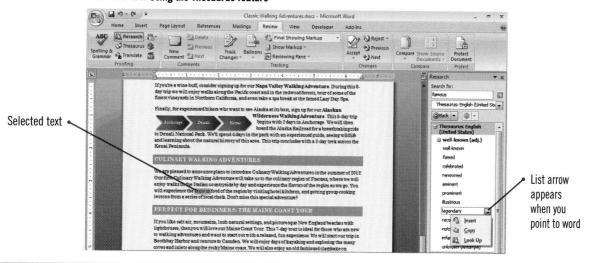

Comparing or viewing multiple documents at once

Word 2007 includes several options for working in multiple documents at once. To compare and combine two versions of a document, click the Compare button in the Compare group of the Review tab. To see all open documents on the screen at once, click the Arrange All button in the window group of the View tab; Word displays each document within an independent tile so that you can work in each window. If you want to work with two similar documents at once, the View Side by Side button in the Window group of the View tab might be a more useful option. It synchronizes the tiled windows so that when you scroll through one document the other scrolls too; this can be great for comparing similar sections in the two files. Or, if you prefer to scroll in one window without scrolling in the other, you can turn this option off by clicking the Synchronous Scrolling button in the Window group.

Learning New Ways to Distribute Documents

In addition to the new XML file format, Office 2007 includes new tools for finalizing and distributing your work electronically, even if the intended audience is not using Word 2007. Word 2003 allowed you save a document in many different file formats, but Word 2007 includes easy-to-find options for saving to PDF or XPS, saving to an earlier version of Word, publishing directly to a blog, and creating a document workspace. A new Quick Print command lets you print directly to the default printer without opening a dialog box. If you are working with others on a document, creating a **document workspace** posts a copy of your document to a URL so that everyone can synchronize their local copy of the file or related files with the server copy. (Use of this feature requires access to the Microsoft Windows SharePoint Services site.) In this lesson prepare your document for publication and print a copy.

STEPS

1. **Click the Office button , then point to Prepare**

   The Prepare submenu opens. You can use the commands on this menu to edit document properties while a document is open, inspect the document for personal information, encrypt it so that it can only be opened by authorized users, add a digital signature, mark it as final so it cannot be edited, or run a compatibility checker to see what elements will be affected if you save to an earlier version of Word.

2. **Click Run Compatibility Checker**

   The Microsoft Office Word Compatibility Checker opens, as shown in Figure B-25. The summary informs you of what changes will be made if you save a copy of this document in an earlier version of Word. Many of the new dynamic features such as content controls and SmartArt graphics, which are not available in earlier versions, will be converted to static elements.

3. **Click OK**

4. **Click , point to Prepare, then click Mark as Final**

   A dialog box opens, informing you that the document will be marked as final and saved. You cannot make any changes to a document marked as final. The purpose of this feature is to prevent any unintentional changes and communicate to others that the document is complete.

   > **QUICK TIP**
   > If you decide you no longer want a document marked as final, click the Office button, point to Prepare, then click Mark as Final to turn this option off.

5. **Click OK, then click OK in the next dialog box**

   A Marked as Final icon appears in the status bar, as shown in Figure B-26.

6. **Scroll up to the beginning of the document, then attempt to delete the word Walking at the beginning of the document**

   A message in the status bar informs you that modifications to the document are not permitted.

7. **Click , then point to Send**

   The Send submenu includes commands for emailing a document (either as an attachment or in the body of the message) or sending it as an Internet fax.

8. **Point to Print, click Print Preview, then click the Two Pages button in the Zoom group on the Print Preview tab**

   As in Word 2003, Print Preview lets you view your document as it will look when printed. The Print Preview tab includes buttons for adjusting margins, paper size, and making other last-minute changes. See Figure B-27.

9. **Click the Print button in the Print group, print one copy of the document, close it, then exit Word**

FIGURE B-25: Microsoft Office Word Compatibility Checker

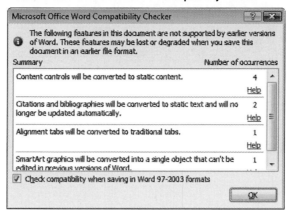

FIGURE B-26: Document is marked as final

Marked as
Final icon

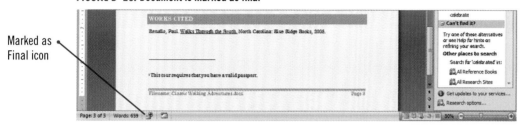

FIGURE B-27: Print Preview window

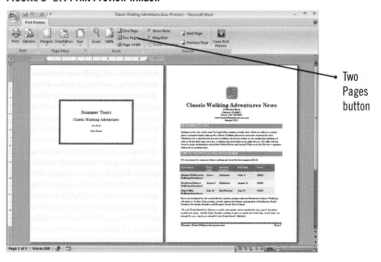

Two
Pages
button

Publishing to a blog

If you are a blogger, you can compose and proof your posts in Word and then publish directly to many popular blog providers, such as Blogger or WordPress. To publish to a blog, save your changes to the document you want to post, click the Office button, point to Publish, then click Blog. If this is the first time you are publishing to a blog, the Register a Blog Account dialog box opens. Click Register Now, then in the New Blog Account dialog box, click the Blog list arrow, then click the blog publisher you use, such as Blogger, then click Next. (If you do not have a blog account, click the I don't have a blog yet link, then create an account.) In the New Blogger Account dialog box, type the User Name and Password for your account. If you want to post pictures to a server, designate the server location. If you have more than one blog registered to your account, select it in the Choose a Blog dialog box. When you are finished, click OK. The blog entry opens in the document window, and the Blog Post tab opens on the Ribbon. To post your entry, click the Publish button in the Blog group. You may be prompted to re-enter your username and password before completing the post.

Practice

▼ CONCEPTS REVIEW

Match the items below with the elements in Figure B-28.

FIGURE B-28

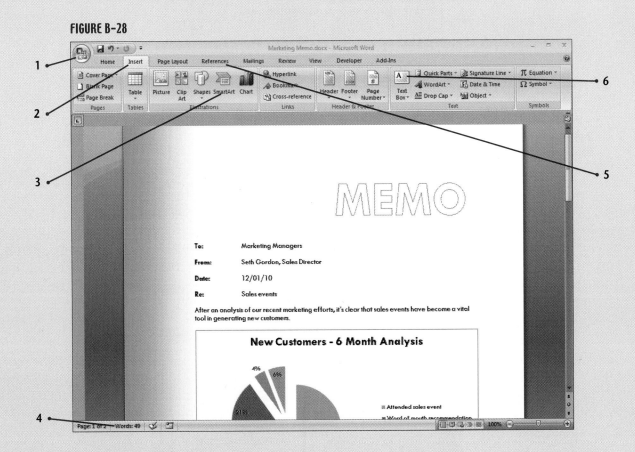

a. Points to the open tab on the Ribbon
b. Points to the button you click to open the Word Count dialog box
c. Points to the button you click to save a text selection as a building block
d. Points to the button you click to create a diagram
e. Points to the tab you click to insert a footnote
f. Points to the Office button

▼ SKILLS REVIEW

1. **Learn new ways to perform tasks in Word.**
   a. Start Word, open the file B-2.doc from the drive and folder where you store your Data Files, then save it as **Studio Info Sheet**.
   b. Use the Go To tab of the Find and Replace dialog box to move to page 4 of the document.
   c. Use a button on the status bar to find out how many paragraphs the document contains.
   d. Move to page 2.
   e. Select the table, then click the Table Tools Design tab.
   f. Apply the Medium Grid 2- Accent 1 Table Style to the table.
   g. Save your changes to the document.

2. **Learn new editing and formatting techniques.**
   a. In the paragraph under Ballet 2, cut the sentence that begins **More step, turn and jump**, then move it to the end of the paragraph so it follows the sentence that ends **move their arms gracefully**.
   b. Click the Replace button in the Editing group on the Home tab, type **Fiesta** in the Find what box, type **Yashenko** in the Replace with box, click Replace All, click OK in the dialog box that informs you that five replacements were made, then click Close in the Find and Replace dialog box.
   c. Move to page 1, then apply the Heading 1 style to the line **About Yashenko Dance Studio**.
   d. Apply the Heading 2 style to the line **Our mission:**.
   e. Add your name at the end of the line that ends **please contact:**.
   f. Change the Style Set for this document to Traditional.
   g. Save your changes to the document.

3. **Learn new page formatting techniques.**
   a. Click the Page Layout tab, then click the Page Borders button.
   b. In the Borders and Shading dialog box click the Box setting, click the Color list arrow, click the Red, Accent 2 color (sixth column, first row under Theme Colors), then click OK.
   c. Apply the Solstice theme to the document.
   d. Click the Orientation button, then click Portrait.
   e. Save your changes to the document.

4. **Learn new ways to work with graphics.**
   a. Click at the end of the phone number line at the top of the document, then press [Enter].
   b. Click the Insert tab on the Ribbon, then click the Clip Art button.
   c. Type **ballet shoes** in the Search for box, verify that All collections appears in the Search in box, click the Results should be list arrow, verify that a check mark appears next to Clip Art, then click Go.

FIGURE B-29

   d. Insert the ballet shoes clip shown in Figure B-29. If this clip is not available, choose a different clip.
   e. Apply the Simple Frame, White Picture Style to the clip.
   f. Close the Clip Art pane.
   g. Move to page 2, click anywhere in the table, position the pointer on the line between the Wednesday column and the Thursday column, then when the pointer changes to ↔, double-click the line to AutoFit the contents the Wednesday column.
   h. Save your changes to the document.

5. **Learn new ways to reuse content.**

   a. Click the Insert tab on the Ribbon, click the Page Number button in the Header & Footer group, point to Bottom of Page, add the built-in Plain Number 2 style under Simple, close the Footer, then save your changes to the document.

   b. Open the file B-3 from the drive and folder where you store your Data Files.

   c. Select the entire paragraph below the heading Studio Mission Statement, click the Insert tab on the Ribbon, click the Text Box button, then click Save Selection to Text Box gallery.

   d. In the Create New Building Block dialog box, type Studio Mission in the Name box, then click OK.

   e. Close the B-3 document without saving changes.

   f. In the Studio Info Sheet document, move to page 1, click at the end of the Our mission: heading, press [Enter], click the Insert tab on the Ribbon, click the Quick Parts button, then click Building Blocks Organizer.

   g. In the Building Blocks Organizer dialog box, scroll down until you see Studio Mission in the Name list, select it, then click Insert.

   h. Verify that the building block was added to the document, then, as a courtesy to other users, open the Building Blocks Organizer and delete the Studio Mission building block entry.

   i. Save your changes to the document.

6. **Learn new ways to add references.**

   a. Click after the clip on page 1, click the References tab on the Ribbon, click the Table of Contents button, then click the Automatic Table 1 style under Built-In.

   b. Move to page 5 of the document, then, in the last sentence, click after the word Life but before the period.

   c. Click the Insert Citation button on the Citations & Bibliography group, notice that one source already exists in this document, then click Add New Source.

   d. In the Create Source dialog box, specify Book as the Type of Source.

   e. Enter Caspar, Calvin as the Author, Dancing for Life as the Title, 2005 as the year, New York as the City, and Valiant Press as the Publisher.

   f. Click the blank line below the heading Books by Our Instructors, click the Bibliography button in the Citations & bibliography group, then click Insert Bibliography (do not choose a Built-In Bibliography style).

   g. Save your changes to the document.

7. **Learn new ways to review documents.**

   a. Click [Ctrl][Home] to move to the beginning of the document.

   b. Use a button on the Review tab to open the Spelling and Grammar dialog box.

   c. As the Spelling Checker flags potential spelling and grammar errors, note the following: Ignore all occurrences of the words Yashenko, Petrushka, Ivana, and barre, and accept the correction to the word lern; accept the suggestion to replace who with that in the sentence about puppets.

   d. Move to page 4, select the text Peter Tchaikovsky, click the Research button, click the All Reference Books list arrow, click Encarta Encyclopedia, then click the Start searching button.

   e. Read the information that appears in the Research pane, including the composer's middle name. Enter the composer's middle name in the document after the word Peter.

   f. Close the Research pane, then save your changes to the document.

8. Learn new ways to distribute documents.

a. Click the Office button, run the Compatibility Checker for this document, read the results, then close the Microsoft Office Word Compatibility Checker dialog box.

b. Mark the document as final.

c. View the document in Print Preview. Pages 1 and 2 of your document should look similar to the document shown in Figure B-30.

d. Print the document, close it, then exit Word.

FIGURE B-30

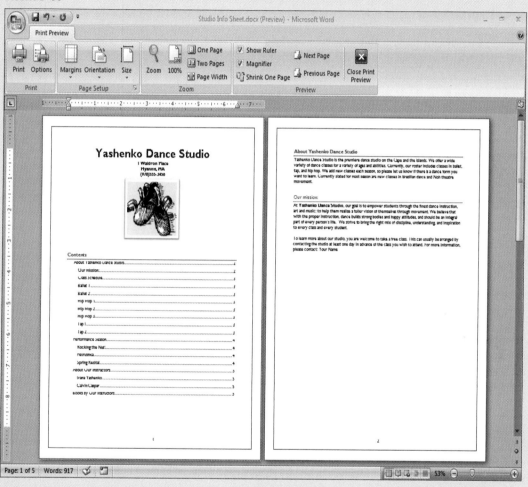

▼ VISUAL WORKSHOP

Use the skills you learned in this unit to create the document shown in Figure B-31. Use the New dialog box to find a template that looks similar to the one shown in the figure, then use the Themes button to change the theme. Save the new document as **City Blooms Fax** to the drive and folder where you store your Data Files. Use a command on the Page Layout tab to add the watermark. Enter your name in the Sender Name content control. Save your changes to the document, print it, close it, then exit Word.

FIGURE B-31

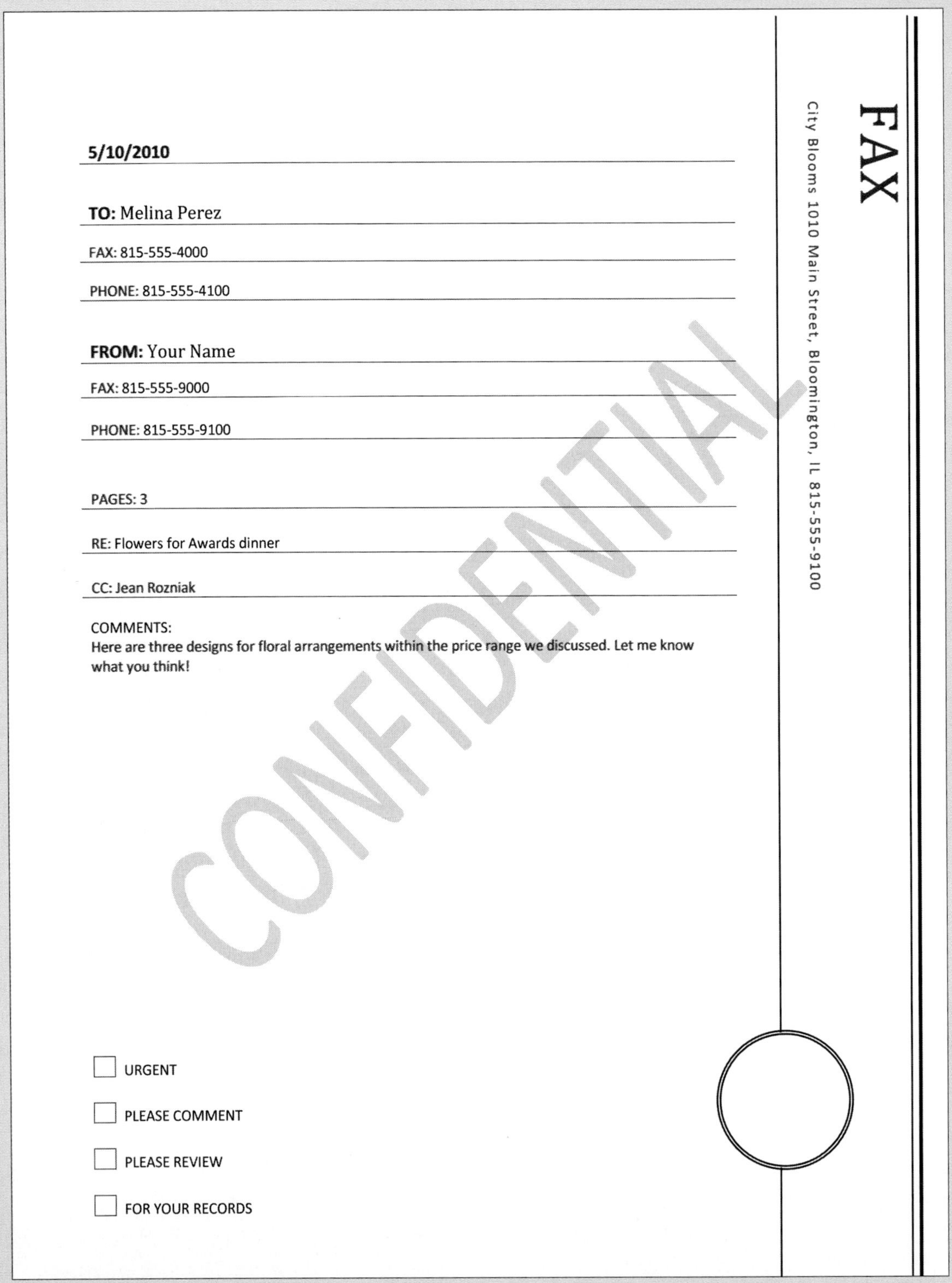

FAX
City Blooms 1010 Main Street, Bloomington, IL 815-555-9100

5/10/2010

TO: Melina Perez

FAX: 815-555-4000

PHONE: 815-555-4100

FROM: Your Name

FAX: 815-555-9000

PHONE: 815-555-9100

PAGES: 3

RE: Flowers for Awards dinner

CC: Jean Rozniak

COMMENTS:
Here are three designs for floral arrangements within the price range we discussed. Let me know what you think!

☐ URGENT

☐ PLEASE COMMENT

☐ PLEASE REVIEW

☐ FOR YOUR RECORDS

Upgrading to Microsoft Office Excel 2007

When you upgrade to Microsoft Office Excel 2007, you will find that the program not only makes it easier to find program commands, but also includes improvements in other areas, such as formatting, formula writing, charting, and data analysis. All of these changes let you create more professional-looking workbooks that present, analyze, and communicate your information faster and more easily than in Microsoft Office Excel 2003. ░░░ In this unit, you will learn the major new features of Excel 2007, and get some hands-on experience by examining and working with sample files.

Objectives

Excel 2007 overview: What's new?

Learn new ways to perform
    program tasks

Learn new themes and styles

Learn new Excel charting features

Learn new conditional
    formatting features

Learn easier ways to type formulas

Learn new table features

Learn new PivotTable
    report features

Learn other new features

Excel 2007 Overview: What's New?

The new Excel 2007 features let you create more visually appealing spreadsheets that make data easier to understand and use. The first thing you will notice in Excel 2007 is the redesigned window: the familiar menus and toolbars are replaced by tabs and buttons. But the changes don't stop there. You can now present, format, and analyze data faster, easier, and with a more professional look. These new features help you better present and communicate your data and the story it has to tell to others. ▰▰▰▰ In this lesson, you will get familiar with the major Excel 2007 features you will learn about in this unit.

DETAILS

As you start to use Excel 2007, you will find changes in the following major program areas:

QUICK TIP

Your screen might not show the Add-Ins tab, depending on the software installed on your computer.

- **New ways to perform program tasks**

  The Excel 2007 window looks quite different from previous versions: the Ribbon tabs replace the familiar menus and toolbars as the principal way you interact with the program. Tab buttons give you one- or two-click access to the most-used Excel features. Figure C-1 contrasts the Excel 2003 and 2007 controls.

- **New formatting options with themes and styles**

  Excel 2003 lets you format worksheets by manually formatting cells and selecting AutoFormats. Excel 2007 gives you a rich array of coordinated formatting options called themes and styles. You can also format cells using cell styles, customize any theme or style, or create your own themes and styles. The Excel 2007 window in Figure C-1 shows a worksheet and chart using the Solstice theme.

- **Professional-looking charts**

  Excel 2007 lets you choose from thousands of formatting combinations to create professional-looking charts. You can easily select chart elements and apply special effects such as shadows, bevels, and soft edges, and base your color combinations on the worksheet theme. As in Excel 2003, you can still customize any element's format. Figure C-1 shows a stacked cylinder chart with theme colors and a bevel effect.

- **Comprehensive conditional formatting**

  Excel 2003 allowed you to create three conditional formatting rules to format data based on its values to help you easily see data trends. In Excel 2007, conditional formatting offers data bars, color scales, and icon sets to highlight data relationships. You can now create up to 64 rules for your data. Figure C-2 shows two types of conditional formatting, an icon set and a color scale.

QUICK TIP

Table styles use Live Preview to let you try out formatting options before you select one.

- **Improved table (formerly list) features**

  In Excel 2003, you used lists to organize data. In Excel 2007, lists are called tables. Excel 2007 tables have several improvements: calculations you create once and automatically apply to an entire column, professionally designed table styles that maintain formatting when you add rows, and a total row that adjusts when you add rows. The table in Figure C-2 displays a total row.

QUICK TIP

If you prefer to enter functions by clicking, the Insert Function dialog box remains unchanged from Excel 2003.

- **Easier formula writing**

  When you typed functions in Excel 2003, you had to remember each function's name and purpose. The Excel 2007 Function AutoComplete feature helps you type functions by providing on-screen help as you type. See Figure C-3.

- **New, easy-to-use PivotTable report interface**

  When you analyzed data using PivotTable reports in Excel 2003, you had to drag and drop fields into an empty PivotTable. In Excel 2007, you use a new PivotTable Field List that contains boxes representing the four PivotTable areas, making it easier to explore data relationships.

- **Other new features**

  Other improvements include a new file format, a new Page Layout view, and increased workbook capacities.

FIGURE C-1: Excel 2003 and Excel 2007 screens

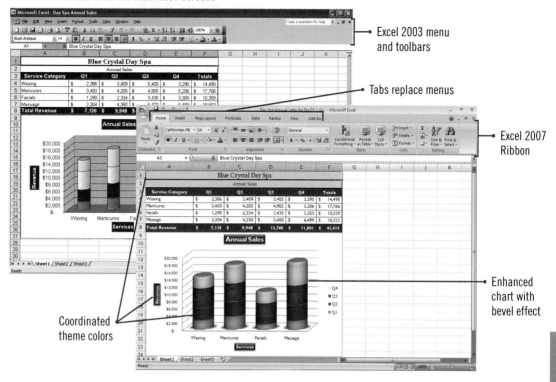

Excel 2003 menu and toolbars

Tabs replace menus

Excel 2007 Ribbon

Enhanced chart with bevel effect

Coordinated theme colors

FIGURE C-2: Conditional formatting based on cell values

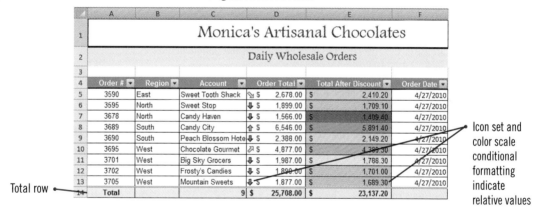

Total row

Icon set and color scale conditional formatting indicate relative values

FIGURE C-3: Function AutoComplete

Function AutoComplete helps you enter the correct function

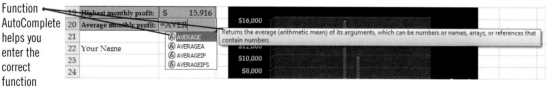

Why the new interface?

You might wonder why Microsoft rearranged Office features. Their research found that over 80% of requests users sent them were for features already in the Office programs! Clearly, users needed more help finding the features they needed. While the menu and toolbar interface worked in earlier program versions, newer features were added over the years. Menus became longer and commands were often "nested" onto submenus, requiring three or four clicks to reach. Some common features became buried in menus and hard to locate. Microsoft decided to overhaul the interface so that you can now access most features in one or two clicks. Now you can accomplish tasks much more quickly than before—making it well worth your while to make the transition.

Learning New Ways to Perform Program Tasks

The most dramatic change in Microsoft Office 2007 is its **new user interface**—the items you click as you interact with the program to get the results you want. Making the transition from using menus and toolbars to using the Ribbon takes a little practice, but you will be rewarded with faster, more intuitive access to the features you use the most. In this lesson, you will examine the new Excel 2007 window layout and practice navigating the new interface.

STEPS

1. **Start Excel, open the file C-1.xlsx from the drive and folder where you store your Data Files, then save it as First Quarter Gift Basket Sales**

   Excel 2007 has a new file format, which uses the file extension .xlsx. The Excel tabs appear in the Ribbon, the Home tab is selected, and the workbook is in Normal view.

   > **QUICK TIP**
   > To temporarily hide the Ribbon, double-click the active tab; click any tab and button to perform an action; double-click any tab to redisplay the Ribbon.

2. **Click the View tab, then click the Page Layout button in the Workbook Views group**

   The workbook appears in the new **Page Layout view** where you can view and edit the header and footer.

3. **Click the text Click to add header, click the File Name button in the Header & Footer Elements group on the Header & Footer Tools Design tab, press [Enter], type your name, then click cell A1 on the worksheet**

   When you work in the header area, the Header & Footer Tools Design tab becomes active. When you click outside the header, you no longer see that tab. Tabs that appear when certain items are selected are called **contextual tabs**. The worksheet name and your name appear in the header, as shown in Figure C-4. You can use either the View tab or the status bar to change views.

4. **Click the Normal button ▦ in the status bar, then click the chart**

   When you select the chart, the Chart Tools contextual tabs appear. They allow you to change the chart's design, layout, and format.

   > **QUICK TIP**
   > If your mouse has a scroll wheel, you can point to the Ribbon, then use the wheel to scroll the tabs.

5. **Click the Chart Tools Design tab, then click the More button ▾ in the Chart Styles group**

   The Chart Styles gallery opens, showing 48 predefined chart styles.

6. **Click the Style 2 design (top row, second from left), then click cell A1**

   You used one of the Chart Tools contextual tabs to change the chart style. The new style has a white background and the pie slices have solid colors instead of gradients.

   > **QUICK TIP**
   > You can use the same keyboard shortcuts in Excel 2007 as you did in Excel 2003.

7. **Select the range E4:E8, click the Conditional Formatting button in the Styles group, point to Data Bars, click the Green Data Bar button, then press [Ctrl][Home]**

   You applied conditional formatting bars to the range. You can quickly distinguish the higher values because they have the longer green bars. See Figure C-5.

8. **Click the Save button 🖫 on the Quick Access toolbar, click the Office button 🔘, point to Print, click Print Preview, click the Print button in the Print group, then click OK**

   Table C-1 summarizes the contents of each tab in the Excel 2007 Ribbon. To find the new command locations in Excel 2007, see the cross-referenced table in the Appendix.

Learning new Excel file formats

Excel 2007 features a new file format: By default, files are now saved with the .xlsx file extension, which is an XML-based format that allows for smaller file sizes, better communication with external data sources, and easier data recovery. The XML format also applies to macro-enabled workbooks, which have an .xlsm file extension, and Excel templates, which have an .xltx extension, and Excel macro-enabled templates, which have a .xltm extension.

FIGURE C-4: Workbook in Page Layout view

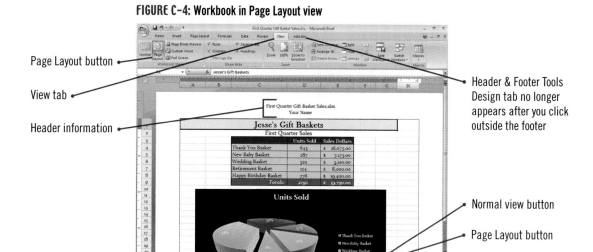

Page Layout button

View tab

Header information

Header & Footer Tools Design tab no longer appears after you click outside the footer

Normal view button

Page Layout button

View buttons on status bar

FIGURE C-5: Green data bars showing relative values

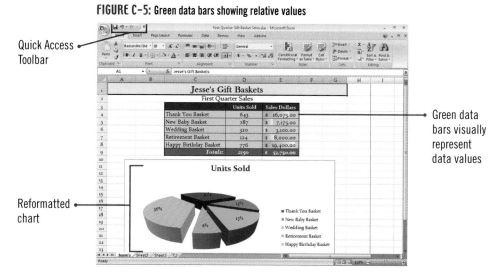

Quick Access Toolbar

Reformatted chart

Green data bars visually represent data values

TABLE C-1: Excel tab summary

tab name	contains information relating to	contains these groups	Office 2003 menu locations
Home	The most commonly used commands in Excel	Clipboard, Font, Alignment, Number, Styles, Cells, Editing	Edit, Format
Insert	Inserting objects into a worksheet	Tables, Illustrations, Charts, Links, Text	Insert, Data
Page Layout	How your data appears on the page	Themes, Page Setup, Scale to Fit, Sheet Options, Arrange	File, Page Setup, View, Format, Window
Formulas	Calculations using formulas and functions	Function Library, Defined Names, Formula Auditing, Calculation	Insert, Tools, Data
Data	Entering, importing, and analyzing data	Get External Data, Connections, Sort & Filter, Data Tools, Outline, Analysis	Tools, Data
Review	Proofing workbooks and collaborating with others	Proofing, Comments, Changes	Insert, Tools
View	Displaying and arranging worksheets, workbooks; working with macros	Workbook Views, Show/Hide, Zoom, Window, Macros	View, Tools, Window
Add-Ins	Varies, depending on installed products	Custom Toolbars	Tools

Learning New Themes and Styles

Excel 2003 allowed you to manually format worksheet elements using commands on the Format menu, including a limited number of AutoFormats. Excel 2007 greatly expands your formatting possibilities through the use of cell styles and themes. **Cell styles** are sets of predefined formatting characteristics, such as fills and fonts. **Themes** are coordinated, predefined sets of colors, fonts, lines, and fills that you can apply to a worksheet. You can use any of the 20 built-in themes, customize a built-in theme, or create your own theme. The same themes are available in Word, Excel, and PowerPoint, allowing you to create a unified look in your Office documents. 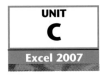 In this lesson, you will practice changing worksheet elements using cell styles and themes.

STEPS

1. **Click the Home tab and cell A1 if necessary, then click the Cell Styles button in the Styles group**

   The Cell Styles gallery opens, displaying several groups of preformatted styles, as shown in Figure C-6. The third group, Titles and Headings, and the fourth group, Themed Cell Styles, use the colors and fonts of the current theme to format cells.

2. **Click Title under Titles and Headings**

   The worksheet title in cell A1 is formatted with the Title cell style. Before you clicked it, Live Preview showed you how the title would look.

3. **Click the Page Layout tab, then point to the Themes button in the Themes group**

   The ScreenTip indicates that the current theme is called Flow.

4. **Click the Themes button**

   The Themes gallery opens, showing built-in themes as well as any custom themes. The Flow theme is highlighted.

5. **Point to the Aspect theme**

   Live Preview shows what your data will look like if you click that option. The filled worksheet areas change to the Aspect theme colors, which are shades of red. The pie slices change to a set of coordinated colors from the Aspect theme. You can try any of the themes, then click the one you like best.

6. **Point to some other available themes, then click the Origin theme**

   After observing how the fills and fonts change for each theme, you decide to apply the Origin theme. This theme changes the worksheet title to Bookman Old Style and the other worksheet and chart text to Gill Sans MT font. The pie chart slices change to colors of the Origin theme.

7. **Click the Colors button in the Themes group, then point to several color options**

   The worksheet and chart colors change though the fonts remain the same. The current theme (in this case, Origin) has a box around it. Each color option contains 12 colors: four text/background colors, six accent colors, and two hyperlink colors. Only eight of the 12 colors appear for each selection on the Colors menu. The face of the Colors button shows the text and background colors for the current theme.

8. **Click anywhere on the worksheet, click the Fonts button in the Themes group, then point to several font options, observing the effect of each one on the worksheet and chart**

   The fonts change though the colors and font sizes remain the same. Some font options use the same font for all the worksheet text, and others use two fonts that go well together. Fonts can be **serif fonts**, which have small lines called serifs at the tops and bottoms of the letters, such as Century Schoolbook and Georgia, or **sans serif fonts**, with no serifs on the letters, such as Aspect and Calibri.

9. **Click the Apex Font style, if necessary click cell A1, compare your screen to Figure C-7, then save and close the workbook**

   The worksheet reflects the theme and font style you chose.

FIGURE C-6: Selecting options from the Cell Styles gallery

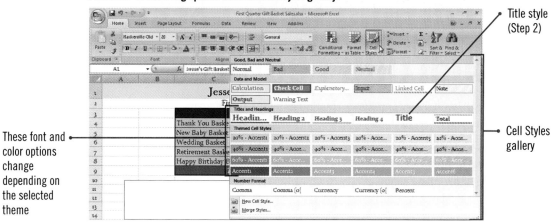

Title style (Step 2)

These font and color options change depending on the selected theme

Cell Styles gallery

FIGURE C-7: Worksheet with new theme and font style

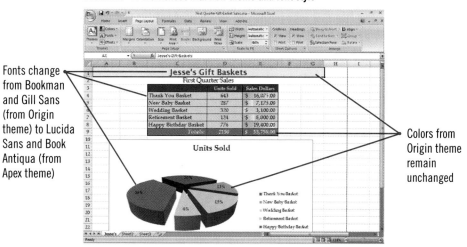

Fonts change from Bookman and Gill Sans (from Origin theme) to Lucida Sans and Book Antiqua (from Apex theme)

Colors from Origin theme remain unchanged

Customizing themes

You can customize theme colors to create your own color combinations. For example, you might want to use the colors in your company logo. To customize theme colors, click the Colors button in the Themes group, click Create New Theme Colors, then select new colors for each of the 12 listed colors. The selected color has a red outline, as shown in Figure C-8. As you select each new color, the sample in the Sample area changes to reflect your choice. To save

your theme so it appears in the Themes gallery, assign it a name in the Name text box, then click Save. Custom themes are automatically saved in the Document Themes folder. If you do not see colors you need in the color palette, click More Colors in the Color palette, and enter Red, Green, and Blue (RGB) values for your colors. (You can obtain RGB values using a graphics program such as Adobe PhotoShop.)

FIGURE C-8: Create New Theme Colors dialog box

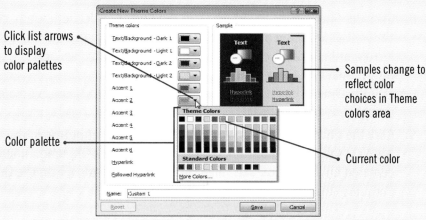

Click list arrows to display color palettes

Color palette

Samples change to reflect color choices in Theme colors area

Current color

Learning New Excel Charting Features

As with worksheet formatting, creating and formatting charts has also undergone major improvements in Excel 2007. You will immediately notice that chart lines look smoother than before, and ClearType fonts display chart text more clearly. An array of chart layouts, chart styles, and shape styles now expands the types of professional-looking charts you can create in just two or three clicks. You can also use themes, and apply many shape effects, such as bevels and transparency. You can easily modify chart elements, such as titles, legends, labels, and axes using the buttons in the Labels and Axes groups. ▰▰▰▰▰ In this lesson, you will create a chart, apply layouts and styles, and customize chart elements.

STEPS

1. **Open the file C-2.xlsx from the drive and folder where you store your Data Files, then save it as** Peter's Walking Tours

2. **Select the range** A4:C10, **click the** Insert tab, **click the** Column button **in the Charts group, click the** 3-D Clustered Column chart button, **then move and resize the chart so it fills the range** A12:D25

   The new chart appears on the worksheet, using the same Trek theme as the worksheet. The Chart Tools Design tab moves to the front.

3. **With the Chart Tools Design tab selected, click the** Chart Styles More button ▾ **in the Chart Styles group, then click** Style 42 (bottom row, second from left), **as shown in Figure C-9**

   > **QUICK TIP**
   > You won't see the chart title text in the placeholder until you press [Enter].

4. **Click the** Chart Tools Layout tab, **click the** Chart Title button **in the Labels group, click the** Centered Overlay Title, **type** Walking Tours 2009-2010, **then press** [Enter]

   > **QUICK TIP**
   > Not all shape effects change the appearance of chart data markers.

5. **Click any 2010 series bar to select the series, click the** Chart Tools Format tab, **click the** Shape Effects button **in the Shape Styles group, point to** Bevel, **observe that the chart style already applied a circle bevel to this bar, then click anywhere on the worksheet**

6. **With the 2010 series still selected, click the** Shape Styles More button ▾, **then click the** Subtle Effect - Accent 1 (fourth row, second from left), **click the** chart title, **then click the** Subtle Effect - Accent 1 style **in the Shape Styles group**

   The 2010 series and the chart title now have coordinated colors.

7. **Click the** Chart Tools Layout tab, **click the** Axes button **in the Axes group, point to** Primary Vertical Axis, **click** Show Axis in Thousands **as shown in Figure C-10, then drag the vertical axis label down to center it on the axis**

   > **QUICK TIP**
   > To add transparency to a chart element, select the element, click the Chart Tools Format tab, click the Shape Fill button in the Shapes Style group, point to Gradient, click More Gradients, click Fill, then click Solid fill or Gradient fill and drag the Transparency slider to the right.

8. **Click the** Chart Elements list arrow **in the Current Selection group, click** Back Wall, **click the** Format Selection button **in the Current Selection group, click** Fill **if necessary, click** Picture or texture fill, **click** File, **navigate to your Data File location, click** C-3.JPG, **click** Insert, **then click** Close

   The Chart Elements list lets you easily select any chart element; you then use the Format Selection button to format the element you selected. The picture appears on the back wall of the chart.

9. **Click the** Chart Tools Design tab, **click the** Move Chart button **in the Location group, click the** New sheet option button, **type** Tours Chart, **click** OK, **drag** Thousands **down so it is centered on the vertical axis, then click the** Save button 🖫 **on the Quick Access toolbar**

   Compare your chart to Figure C-11.

FIGURE C-9: Chart Tools Design options

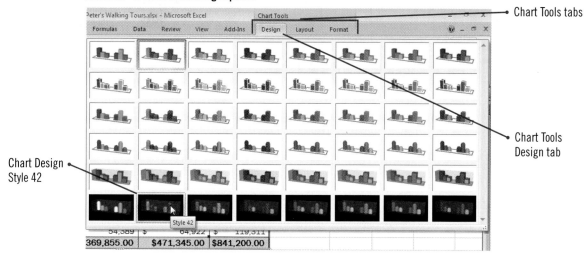

Chart Tools tabs

Chart Tools Design tab

Chart Design Style 42

FIGURE C-10: Modifying the vertical axis with Charts Tools Layout tab

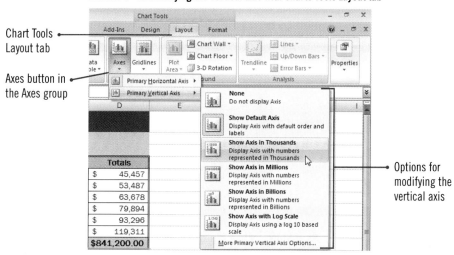

Chart Tools Layout tab

Axes button in the Axes group

Options for modifying the vertical axis

FIGURE C-11: Completed chart

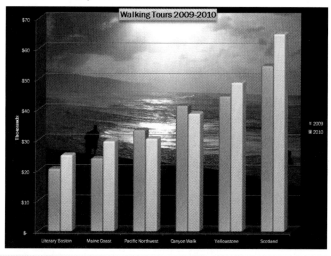

Using Excel charts in other Office programs

Because charting throughout Office 2007 uses Excel, rather than Microsoft Graph, you can now exchange charts easily among the Office programs and link charts to external data sources. As with Office 2003, you can link or embed charts in a file. When you copy and paste an Excel chart into a Word or PowerPoint file, Office 2007 now links the chart by default. You can still embed a chart using the Insert Object command in the Text group on the Insert tab or by using Copy/Paste Special/Paste/As Microsoft Office Excel Chart Object.

Learning New Conditional Formatting Features

Conditional formatting visually indicates the relative values of cell contents. Excel 2003 had conditional formatting, but it was limited both in the number of rules and in the type of formatting it supported. You could use only cell borders and either solid or patterned cell fills for formatting. Excel 2007 allows more rules, and conditional formatting options include icons, data bars, color scales, and icon sets. ▰▰▰ In this lesson you will explore the conditional formatting options in Excel 2007.

STEPS

1. **Click the Tours sheet tab, type your name in cell E30, then drag to select the range B5:C10**

   You want to see how cell values relate to each other graphically.

2. **Click the Home tab, click the Conditional Formatting button in the Styles group, point to Data Bars, then point to the Light Blue Data Bar button**

   The cells fill with varying levels of blue shading. You want to determine what rule Excel used to fill the cells.

3. **Move the mouse pointer down, then click More Rules at the bottom of the menu**

   The New Formatting Rule dialog box opens, shown in Figure C-12, with the rule "Format all cells based on their values" highlighted under "Select a Rule Type." Under Edit the Rule Description, you see that the Data Bar Format Style is selected, and that the shortest bar represents the lowest value and the longest bar the highest.

4. **Click Cancel, click the Conditional Formatting button again, point to Color Scales, point to several color scale options, note how the three-color scales are applied to the data, point to Icon Sets, click the 3 Signs option (right column, third row), then click any blank worksheet cell**

   Compare your worksheet to Figure C-13. The lower values are marked by red diamonds, the middle values have yellow triangles, and the top values have green circles. By default, Excel divided the values into thirds. For the Totals column, you decide to set a rule that will give you more control over how the items are marked. You decide to use cell fills and font colors to format values that are above and below the average value in the range.

5. **Select the range D5:D10, click the Conditional Formatting button, point to Top/Bottom Rules, then click Above Average**

   The Above Average dialog box opens, where you can select a format for above-average values in the range.

6. **Click the list arrow, select Green Fill with Dark Green Text, compare your screen with Figure C-14, then click OK**

   Values that are above the selected range's average appear in green type with a green background.

7. **Click the Conditional Formatting button, point to Top/Bottom Rules, click Below Average, click the list arrow, click Custom Format, click the Fill tab, click the rightmost color in the third row (a light tan), click OK, then click OK**

   The below-average numbers have tan shading. You decide instead to use a rule that marks values under and over $80,000 in total revenue.

8. **Click the Conditional Formatting button, point to Clear Rules, then click Clear Rules from Selected Cells**

9. **Click the Conditional Formatting button, point to Highlight Cells Rules, click Greater Than, type 80000, click the list arrow, click Green Fill with Dark Green Text, click OK, press [Ctrl][Home], compare your screen to Figure C-15, then print, save, and close the file**

Upgrading to Excel 2007

FIGURE C-12: Formatting Rule for blue data bars

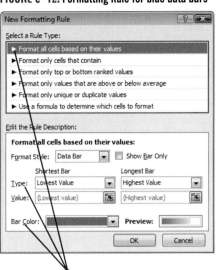

Blue bars assigned to all
values from lowest to highest

FIGURE C-13: Values formatted with icon sets

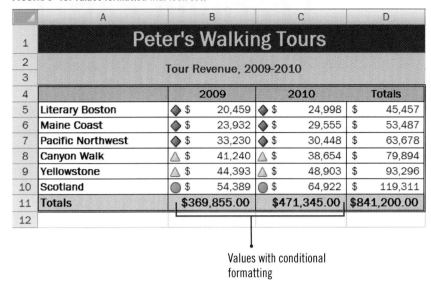

Values with conditional
formatting

FIGURE C-14: Conditionally formatting above-average values

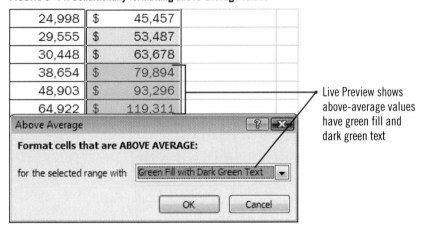

Live Preview shows
above-average values
have green fill and
dark green text

FIGURE C-15: Conditionally formatted worksheet

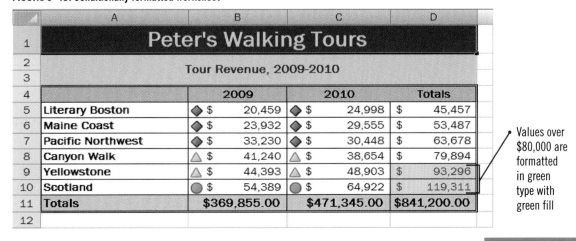

Values over
$80,000 are
formatted
in green
type with
green fill

Learning Easier Ways to Type Formulas

When you type formulas and functions, you need to be especially careful not to introduce errors. That is why Excel introduced the Function Arguments dialog box. However, typing is often the most direct method, especially for experienced users. To assist you, Excel 2007 provides **Function AutoComplete**, which features onscreen help and prompts that guide you to enter the correct arguments for functions you type. █████ In this lesson you will enter some functions to experience the Excel AutoComplete feature for yourself.

STEPS

1. **Open the file** C-4.xls **from the drive and folder where you store your Data Files, save it as** Western Region Sales, **then scroll down to view the range** A25:B32

> **QUICK TIP**
>
> To write a long, mul-tiline formula, click the Expand Formula Bar button ⌄ to write up to three lines. For formulas longer than three lines, use the scroll arrows on the right side of the bar.

2. **Click cell** B27, **then type** =A

The Function AutoComplete menu appears, as well as an onscreen help box that shows the purpose of the selected function at the top of the list, ABS. See Figure C-16.

3. **Type** V

The list of available functions shortens to include only those that start with AV, and the help box now describes the AVEDEV function at the top of the list.

4. **Press** [down arrow key]

The AVERAGE function is selected, and its description appears in the help box.

5. **Press** [Tab]

The AVERAGE function appears in cell B27. As in Excel 2003, a ScreenTip shows the function name and the argument prompts in parentheses, ready for you to type or drag a range reference.

6. **Drag to select the range** F4:F7, **then press** [Enter]

Excel enters the final parenthesis, and the average for Gordon, 16,762, appears in cell B27.

> **QUICK TIP**
>
> As you type an argument, AutoComplete lists both functions and names defined for your workbook, so you can easily per-form calculations with named ranges, such as SUM(Bob_Sales).

7. **With cell** B28 **selected, type** =AVER, **press** [Tab], **drag to select** F8:F12, **then press** [Enter]

8. **Repeat Step 7 to enter the average for Wiley in cell** B29 **(use the range** F13:F15**) and for Emerson in cell** B30 **(use the range** F16:F22**)**

9. **In cell** B31, **type** =MAX, **press** [Tab], **drag to select the range** D4:E22, **press** [Enter]**; in cell** B32, **type** =MIN, **press** [Tab], **drag to select the range** D4:E22, **click the** Enter **button** ✓ **on the for-mula bar, compare your screen to Figure C-17, enter your name in cell** A34, **then save the file**

FIGURE C-16: Function AutoComplete list and help box

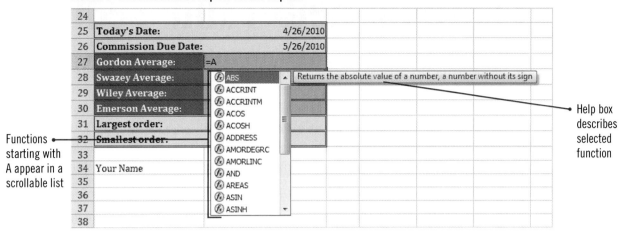

Functions starting with A appear in a scrollable list

Help box describes selected function

FIGURE C-17: Completed formulas

24			
25	Today's Date:		4/26/2010
26	Commission Due Date:		5/26/2010
27	Gordon Average:	$	16,762
28	Swazey Average:	$	7,497
29	Wiley Average:	$	9,484
30	Emerson Average:	$	7,694
31	Largest order:	$	26,222
32	Smallest order:	$	234
33			

Using the new Name Manager dialog box

In Excel 2003, you created and managed names using several selections on the Insert/Name submenu. In Excel 2007, you manage names in the Defined Names group on the Formulas tab. The Name Manager dialog box now lets you create new names, edit existing names, and delete them, all in one location. In addition, you can specify a range's **scope**, which is the location in which Excel recognizes the range name, as either the worksheet or the workbook. The Name Manager dialog box has a Filter button that lets you view all defined names, names scoped to the worksheet, names scoped to the workbook, or table names. You can clear the filter to display all names. See Figure C-18.

FIGURE C-18: Name Manager dialog box with Filter menu

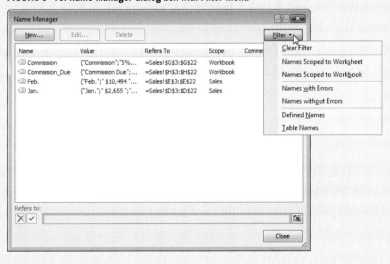

Learning New Table Features

UNIT
C

Excel 2007

In Excel 2003, you used lists to organize, sort, and filter structured data, which has the same type of information in each column, such as customer or inventory lists. In Excel 2007, a list is now called a **table**, and you will find it easier to use because of additional features. If you add a column with a formula to the column on the right side of a table, the **calculated column** feature copies it to the entire column. **Table styles** automatically format additional rows, and the table total row lets you choose a variety of functions for any column. Excel 2007 no longer supports the data form feature found in Excel 2003. In this lesson you will use an Excel table to analyze sales representatives' performance data, which has rows of similarly structured data.

STEPS

1. **Press [Ctrl][Home], click anywhere in the range A4:H22, click the Insert tab, then click the Table button in the Tables group**

   The Create Table dialog box opens, suggesting the range $A$3:$H$22 for your table, as shown in Figure C-19. The range is correct.

2. **Verify that the My table has headers check box is checked, click OK, then click anywhere in the table**

   The data is now formatted as a table, with AutoFilter list arrows on each column header, and a table style applied to it. The Table Tools Design tab opens in the Ribbon and moves to the front. See Figure C-20.

> **QUICK TIP**
>
> To select only the cells in a table row or column, right-click any cell, point to Select, then click Entire Table Column (which includes the header and total row) or Table Row. Selecting Table Column Data includes the column data but not the header or total row.

3. **Click the More button ▼ in the Table Styles group, point to several styles in the Light, Medium, and Dark areas, then click Table Style Medium 4 style (first Medium row, fourth from left)**

4. **Click the Sales Rep list arrow, click (Select All) to remove the check marks, click the check boxes for Judy Wiley and Tyler Gordon to select them, then click OK**

   You filtered the table to show only the records for Judy Wiley and Tyler Gordon. AutoFiltering is turned on by default in Excel 2007.

5. **Point to the small triangle in the table's lower-right corner until the pointer becomes ↘, drag to the right one column to extend the table to column I, click cell I6, type =, then click cell F6**

   The first formula cell reference appears as a **structured reference**, which includes the default table name and a cell reference that includes the row [This Row] and column [Total] designation.

> **QUICK TIP**
>
> You can enter a formula for a calculated column in any table row.

6. **Type *.06, then press [Enter]**

   The calculated column feature enters the formula in all the other rows in the table in column I.

7. **Click the Column1 header, type If 6%, then press [Enter]**

   With a table cell selected, you can easily display a total row.

> **QUICK TIP**
>
> Editing a formula in a calculated column changes all the other formulas in that column. See Excel online help for a listing of exceptions to this rule. You can use the AutoCorrect Option list arrow to undo calculated columns or turn off the feature.

8. **On the Table Tools Design tab, click to select Total Row in the Table Style Options group, click cell I23, click its list arrow, then click Count**

   The total row appears and displays a total in cell I23. The selected cell's list arrow lets you choose from a list of functions. Cell I23 indicates that there are seven items in the current filtered table.

9. **Click the Sales Rep list arrow, then click Clear Filter From "Sales Rep"**

   The count in cell I23 indicates there are 19 items in the unfiltered table.

10. **Select cells I4:I22, right-click the range, click the Accounting Number Format button $ on the Mini toolbar, click the Decrease Decimal button twice, point to any table cell, compare your screen to Figure C-21, then save and close the file**

Upgrading to Excel 2007

FIGURE C-19: Create Table dialog box

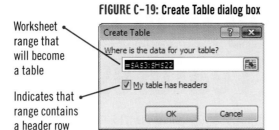

Worksheet range that will become a table

Indicates that range contains a header row

FIGURE C-20: Table with Table Tools Design tab

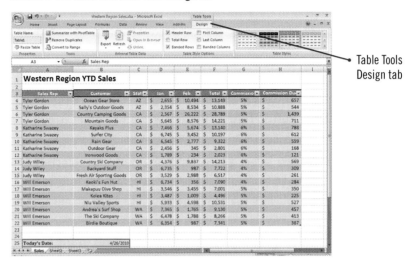

Table Tools Design tab

FIGURE C-21: Completed table

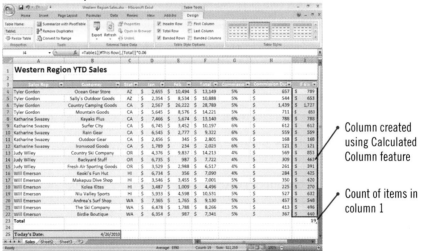

Column created using Calculated Column feature

Count of items in column 1

Using structured references

Excel 2007 table formulas refer to table cells using structured references, which use names instead of cell references. For example, when you create a table formula that you would otherwise write as =C4-C3, Excel enters these references using the row and column name, such as =Table1[[#This Row],[February]]-Table1[[#This Row],[Sales Rep]:[January]]. Although they might look more complex at first, structured references not only make table formulas easier to read once you get used to them, they make it easier to work with table formulas when you update table data over time; structured references change automatically. You don't have to manually adjust formula ranges when you add records. Structured references are also useful when you use Formula AutoComplete because they use the default table name, which is Table1. You can change the table name in the Properties group on the Table Tools Design tab. Select the table name, type a new one, then press [Enter]. The table name also appears in the Name Manager dialog box. Structured column references refer to only the table data, not including the header or total rows. For complete information on structured references, including syntax rules and information about copying them to different locations, see Excel 2007 online help.

Learning New PivotTable Report Features

Excel 2007 PivotTable reports, often called PivotTables for short, are used for summarizing similarly structured data and are easier to use than those in Excel 2003. In Excel 2007, the Field List now fills the right side of the screen, and it has a **layout section**, four boxes that function as drop areas for fields you want to add to the PivotTable. PivotTable styles also let you quickly apply a professional-looking design. ▰▰▰ In this lesson, you will create a PivotTable and a PivotChart.

STEPS

1. **Open the file C-5.xlsx from the location where you store your Data Files, save it as 2009 Sales; click anywhere in the columns of data, click the Insert tab, then click the PivotTable button (not its list arrow) in the Tables group**
   The Create PivotTable dialog box opens, shown in Figure C-22.

2. **Verify that the Select a table or range button is selected, that the highlighted range is Sales!$A$2:$E$74, and that the New Worksheet option button is selected, then click OK**
   See Figure C-23. When you move a field from the Field List into a box in the layout section, the data moves into the corresponding area of the PivotTable report on the left.

3. **Click the Category and Sales field check boxes in the PivotTable Field List**
   The Category field moves into the Row Labels field and the Sales field moves to the Values area by default. On the PivotTable, the three product categories appear in rows 4, 5, and 6; the total sales for each category appear in the Sum of Sales area, as well as a Grand Total. If you click only a field name check box to select it, Excel moves it to its default location. Nonnumeric fields move to the Row Labels area and numeric fields move to the Values area, but you can move them to other areas.

4. **Click the Office field check box in the PivotTable Field List**
   The Office field moves into the Row Labels area. On the PivotTable, the sales for each product category appear by state. You decide you want the Office locations to appear as column headings.

5. **Click the Office field in the layout section of the Field List, then in the shortcut menu, click Move to Column Labels**
   The Report Filter area allows you to investigate how the sales break down by quarter.

6. **In the PivotTable Field List, right-click the Quarter field, then click Add to Report Filter**
   The Quarter field moves to the Report Filter area above the PivotTable.

7. **On the PivotTable, click the Quarter list arrow, click 1, click OK, click the Undo button ↺ on the Quick Access toolbar, click the Quarter list arrow again, click 2, then click OK**
   Excel 2007 lets you undo PivotTable steps. The PivotTable now displays 2nd quarter data.

8. **Click the PivotTable Tools Design tab, click the More button ▾ in the PivotTable Styles group, click the Pivot Style Dark 16, click the PivotTable Tools Options tab, click Field Settings in the Active Field group, click Number Format, click the Currency category, change the number of decimal places to 0, then click OK twice**

9. **On the PivotTable Tools Options tab, click the PivotChart button in the Tools group, click the 3-D Clustered Column button (top row, fourth from the left), then click OK**
   The PivotChart appears, showing the data for the second quarter.

10. **On the PivotChart Filter Pane, click the Report Filter list arrow, click (All), then click OK; drag the PivotChart below the PivotTable, enter your name in cell A28, click the PivotChart, compare your screen to Figure C-24, print the sheet, then save and close the file**

FIGURE C-22: Create PivotTable dialog box

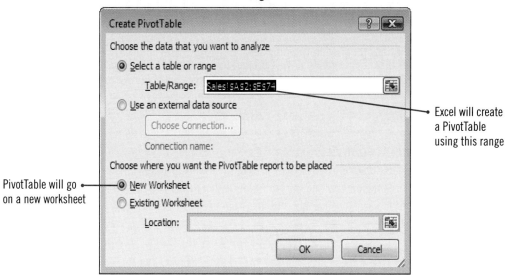

Excel will create a PivotTable using this range

PivotTable will go on a new worksheet

FIGURE C-23: Empty PivotTable and PivotTable Fields List

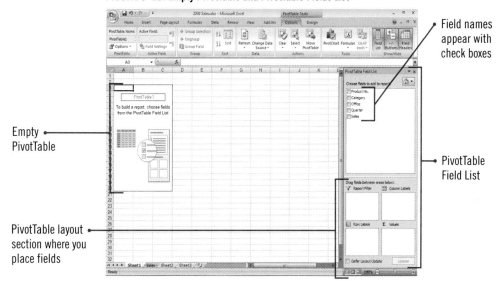

Field names appear with check boxes

Empty PivotTable

PivotTable Field List

PivotTable layout section where you place fields

FIGURE C-24: PivotTable with style and number formats applied

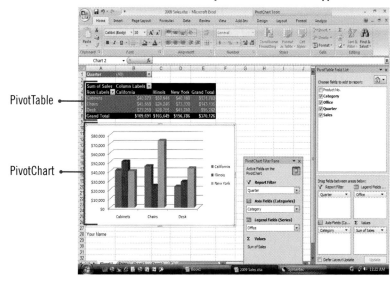

PivotTable

PivotChart

Learning Other New Features

Excel 2007 includes other program upgrades, many of which will help display and analyze your data more effectively and efficiently. ▉▉▉▉ In this lesson you will review some other new features of Excel 2007.

As you use Excel 2007, note these additional features:

- **New Page Layout view**

  This new view accurately represents what your worksheet will look like when printed. You can change margins, headers, and footers and move charts and other objects where you want them. In conjunction with the Page Layout tab, where you can easily change important options such as page orientation, page breaks, and titles that print on every page, you now have one- or two-click access to many of the features you will use the most. Figure C-25 shows the Page Layout tab with the worksheet in Page Layout view.

- **Increased capacity**

  Excel 2007 has a great deal more capacity in many areas, from the number of worksheet rows and columns to the number of unique colors and sort levels. See Table C-2 for a comparison of selected program capacities.

- **PDF using add-ins**

  To create a Portable Document Format (PDF) file from an Excel document, you need to use an add-in program. To find it, search Excel online help for "PDF add-in," click the link for "Enable support for other file formats, such as PDF and XPS," then follow the instructions.

- **Compatibility with earlier versions**

  If you want to use Excel 2007 files in earlier versions of Excel, you can save them using the Excel 97-2003 Workbook (*.xls) format. When you do this, Excel presents a dialog box identifying any 2007 features that cannot be preserved in the earlier format. If a user does not have Excel 2007, the user can still open an Excel 2007 file if a file converter was downloaded.

  When you open a workbook created in an earlier version, Excel 2007 opens it in the new **Compatibility Mode**, which disables the newer 2007 features. That way, you cannot use features that will present problems when other users try to open it in an earlier version. The **Compatibility Checker** finds any issues and lets you create a report so you can resolve the issues. Click the Office button, click Prepare, then click Run Compatibility Checker.

- **New SmartArt graphics**

  While Excel 2003 featured a number of diagrams and organizational charts, Excel 2007 offers SmartArt graphics with a dramatically new look. On the Insert tab, click SmartArt in the Illustrations group, which opens the SmartArt Graphic gallery. Here you can choose many variations of list, process, cycle, hierarchy, relationship, matrix, and pyramid graphic types. You can also choose special effects for drawn objects using the Shape Effects button in the Shape Styles group on the Drawing Tools Format tab. Figure C-26 shows samples of three types of SmartArt graphics.

- **Excel Services to share spreadsheets**

  Excel Services is a new server technology included in Office 2007. This technology allows loading, displaying, and calculating Excel spreadsheets on servers (computers on networks that manage files). Users on the network can access data stored on the server. A manager might create a spreadsheet, then save it to a SharePoint document library on a server. Another manager can use a browser to view the SharePoint document library and click a link to the spreadsheet, which connects to a browser-based version of the spreadsheet.

- **What's gone**

  With all the new Excel 2007 features, it was inevitable that other features would be discontinued. In addition to deleting the data form in tables, Microsoft also eliminated the Office Assistant and interactive Web pages, and retired some older file formats in the Open and Save dialog boxes.

FIGURE C-25: Workbook in Page Layout view

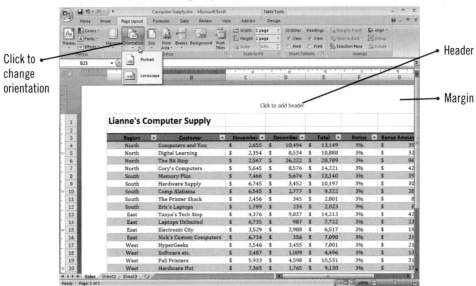

FIGURE C-26: SmartArt graphics

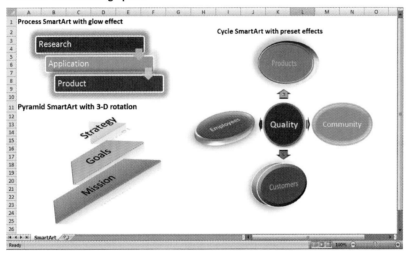

TABLE C-2: Excel 2007 increased capacities

program area	Excel 2003	Excel 2007
Number of columns	256	16,384
Number of rows	65,536	1,048,576
Number of colors	56	16 million
Number of sort levels	3	64
Number of characters in a formula	1,024	8,192
Number of nested levels in formulas	7	64
Number of arguments in a function	30	255
Number of conditional formats	3	Limited only by memory

Practice

If you have a SAM user profile, you may have access to hands-on instruction, practice, and assessment of the skills covered in this unit. Log in to your SAM account (http://sam2007.course.com/) to launch any assigned training activities or exams that relate to the skills covered in this unit.

▼ CONCEPTS REVIEW

Label each of the elements shown in Figure C-27.

FIGURE C-27

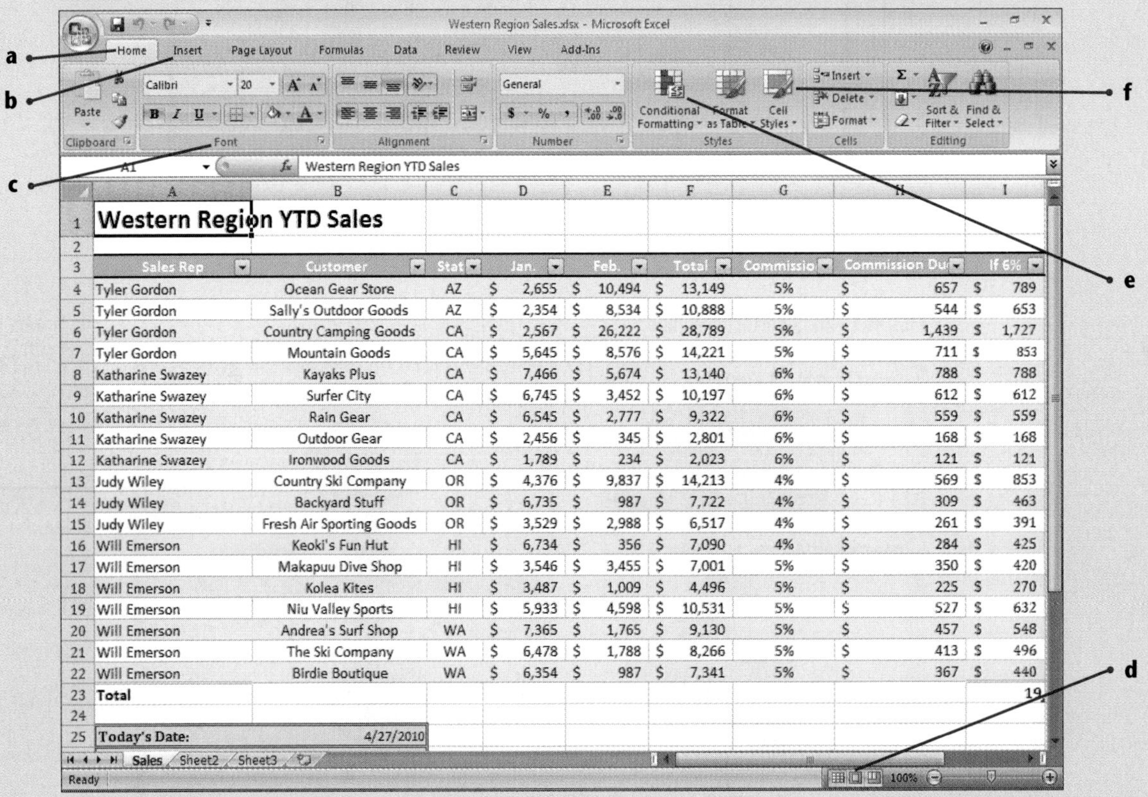

1. Which element points to a group?
2. What is the first element you click when you want to place a table or a chart in your worksheet?
3. Which element contains the most commonly used features in Excel?
4. Which element do you click to format cells a particular way based on the value the cell contains?
5. Which element changes the worksheet view so you can see worksheet headers and footers?
6. Which element do you click to apply a predetermined format to a cell?

▼ SKILLS REVIEW

1. Learn new ways to perform program tasks.

   a. Start Excel, open the file C-6.xlsx from the drive and folder where you store your Data Files, then save it as British Imports.

   b. Use the View tab to view the file in Page Layout view.

   c. Add your name to the center of the header, then use the status bar to redisplay the sheet in Normal view.

   d. Select the chart.

   e. Use the Chart Tools Design tab to assign Style 46 to the chart.

   f. Select the range B5:B16, then use the Conditional Formatting feature to assign the Red - Yellow - Green Color Scale.

   g. Move the chart below that data, then save the worksheet.

2. Learn new themes and styles.

   a. Select the range G5:G16, then apply the themed cell style 40% - Accent 4.

   b. Use the Page Layout tab to apply the Apex theme.

   c. Apply the Office color scheme.

   d. Print the worksheet, compare your printout to Figure C-28, then save and close the file. (*Note*: Don't be concerned if the vertical axis increments in Print Preview are larger than they are on the worksheet.)

3. Learn new Excel charting features.

   a. Open the file C-7.xlsx from the drive and folder where you store your Data Files, then save it as Hironaka Sales.

   b. Create a clustered cylinder chart using the data in A4:C10.

   c. Use the Chart Tools Design tab to apply Chart Style 3 to the chart.

   d. Use the Chart Tools Layout tab to add a chart title above the chart.

   e. Enter the title Hironaka Sales.

   f. Use the Shape Effects button on the Chart Tools Format tab to apply a Circle bevel to both data series.

   g. Use the Chart Tools Layout tab to show the vertical axis in thousands. (*Hint*: Use the Axes button in the Axes group.) Center the word Thousands on the vertical axis.

   h. Use the Chart Elements list arrow in the Current Selection group to select the chart's back wall, then use the Format Selection button to add a Picture fill using the file C-8.jpg.

   i. Use the Chart Tools Design tab to move the chart to its own sheet titled Sales Chart, then center the Thousands text.

4. Learn new conditional formatting features.

   a. Return to the Sales sheet.

   b. Select the range B5:C10, open the New Formatting Rule dialog box for color scales, then observe the current rule description.

   c. Change the color of the minimum value to Light yellow, Background 2, and the maximum value to Brown, Accent 2.

   d. Select the range D5:D10, then use the Highlight Cell Rules submenu to format values greater than 100,000 with red text.

   e. Clear the rule from D5:D10, then format the values using the icon set 3 Traffic Lights (Unrimmed).

   f. Add your name in cell A30, print the worksheet, compare your printout to Figure C-29, then save and close the file.

FIGURE C-28

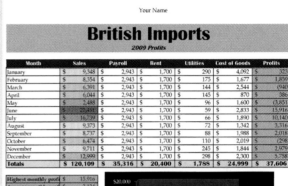

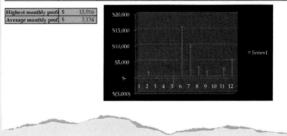

FIGURE C-29

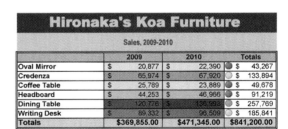

5. **Learn easier ways to type formulas.**
   a. Open the file C-9.xlsx from the drive and folder where you store your Data Files, then save it as **Computer Supply**.
   b. Scroll down to view the range A25:B31.
   c. Select cell B26, type =COU, then use [Tab] to display the Function AutoComplete ScreenTip.
   d. Drag to enter the range G4:G7, then enter the formula.
   e. Use the same procedure to obtain the count for the South region, using the range G8:G12.
   f. Repeat step e for the East region using the range G13:G16, and for the West region using the range G17:G22.
   g. In cell B30, enter the MAX function using the Function AutoComplete feature to find the largest bonus in column G.
   h. In cell B31, enter the MIN function using the Function AutoComplete feature to find the smallest bonus in column G.

6. **Learn new table features.**
   a. Scroll to the top of the worksheet, click in the data range, then insert a table using the appropriate range, including table headers.
   b. Use the Table Tools Design tab to apply Table Style Medium 16 to the table.
   c. Filter the table to display only the East and West regions.
   d. Clear the filter.
   e. Drag to enlarge the table one column to the right.
   f. Choose any appropriate cell in column H and enter a formula that multiplies the Bonus Amount times 2, then verify that the formula was automatically copied to the appropriate range.
   g. Change the Column1 header to **Double**.
   h. Use a table style option to add a total row to the table.
   i. Click in the total cell and change the function to an average.
   j. Format the range H4:H23 with the Accounting format with zero decimal places. (*Hint*: Right-click the selected range and use the Mini toolbar.)
   k. Click cell A23 and type **Average**, then add your name to cell A32. (*Hint*: If cell A32 takes on the format of the cells above it, use the Format Painter to paste the format from cell A23 to cell A32.)
   l. Open the Page Setup dialog box by clicking the Page Setup launcher on the Page Layout tab, fit the worksheet to 1 page wide by 1 page tall in landscape orientation, print the worksheet and compare your printout to Figure C-30, then save and close the workbook.

FIGURE C-30

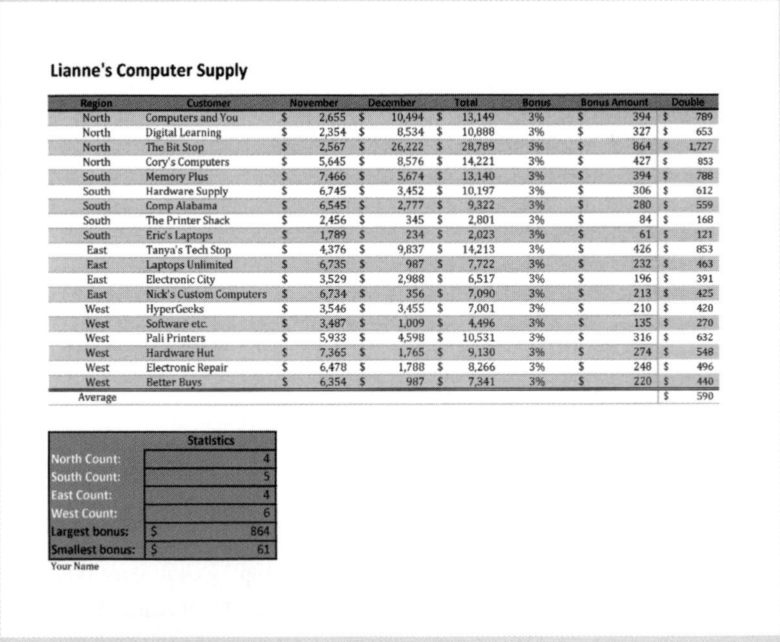

Lianne's Computer Supply

Region	Customer	November	December	Total	Bonus	Bonus Amount	Double
North	Computers and You	$ 2,655	$ 10,494	$ 13,149	3%	$ 394	$ 789
North	Digital Learning	$ 2,354	$ 8,534	$ 10,888	3%	$ 327	$ 653
North	The Bit Stop	$ 2,567	$ 26,222	$ 28,789	3%	$ 864	$ 1,727
North	Cory's Computers	$ 5,645	$ 8,576	$ 14,221	3%	$ 427	$ 853
South	Memory Plus	$ 7,466	$ 5,674	$ 13,140	3%	$ 394	$ 788
South	Hardware Supply	$ 6,745	$ 3,452	$ 10,197	3%	$ 306	$ 612
South	Comp Alabama	$ 6,545	$ 2,777	$ 9,322	3%	$ 280	$ 559
South	The Printer Shack	$ 2,456	$ 345	$ 2,801	3%	$ 84	$ 168
South	Eric's Laptops	$ 1,789	$ 234	$ 2,023	3%	$ 61	$ 121
East	Tanya's Tech Stop	$ 4,376	$ 9,837	$ 14,213	3%	$ 426	$ 853
East	Laptops Unlimited	$ 6,735	$ 987	$ 7,722	3%	$ 232	$ 463
East	Electronic City	$ 3,529	$ 2,988	$ 6,517	3%	$ 196	$ 391
East	Nick's Custom Computers	$ 6,734	$ 356	$ 7,090	3%	$ 213	$ 425
West	HyperGeeks	$ 3,546	$ 3,455	$ 7,001	3%	$ 210	$ 420
West	Software etc.	$ 3,487	$ 1,009	$ 4,496	3%	$ 135	$ 270
West	Pali Printers	$ 5,933	$ 4,598	$ 10,531	3%	$ 316	$ 632
West	Hardware Hut	$ 7,365	$ 1,765	$ 9,130	3%	$ 274	$ 548
West	Electronic Repair	$ 6,478	$ 1,788	$ 8,266	3%	$ 248	$ 496
West	Better Buys	$ 6,354	$ 987	$ 7,341	3%	$ 220	$ 440
Average							$ 590

Statistics		
North Count:		4
South Count:		5
East Count:		4
West Count:		6
Largest bonus:	$	864
Smallest bonus:	$	61
Your Name		

7. Learn new PivotTable report features.

   a. Open the file C-10.xlsx from the drive and folder where you store your Data Files, then save it as **Expense Report**.

   b. Insert a PivotTable report on a separate worksheet using the data.

   c. Click the Date check box so the field moves to the Row Labels area.

   d. Right-click the Item field and add it to the Column Labels area.

   e. Add the Amount field to the Values area.

   f. Click the Item field in the Column Labels area, then click Remove Field.

   g. Right-click the Destination field, then move it to the Column Labels area.

   h. Click the Date field in the Row Labels area, then remove it from the PivotTable.

   i. Move the Item field to the Column Labels area, then undo the action.

   j. Move the Item field to the Row Labels area.

   k. Apply Pivot Style Medium 5 to the PivotTable.

   l. Use the Field Settings button on the PivotTable Tools Options tab to open the Value Field Settings dialog box, then change the number format to Accounting with zero decimal places.

  m. Use the appropriate button on the PivotTable Tools Options tab to create a PivotChart using the 3-D Cone chart type.

   n. Center the PivotChart under the data, view it in Page Layout view, scroll up if necessary and add your name to the header, click in a blank area of the worksheet, return to Normal view, print the sheet and compare your printout to Figure C-31, then save and close the file.

FIGURE C-31

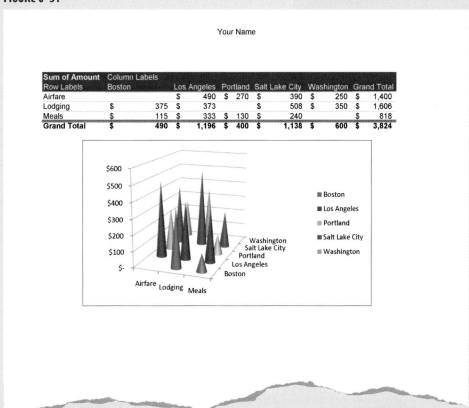

▼ VISUAL WORKSHOP

Open the file C-11.xlsx from the drive and folder where you store your Data Files, then save it as **Ski Packages**. Create the PivotTable report shown in Figure C-32, using PivotStyle Dark 19, and formatting the data as shown. Create the PivotChart, apply Style 46, and position it as shown. Deselect the PivotChart, add your name to the sheet header, print the worksheet with the PivotTable and PivotChart, then save and close the file.

FIGURE C-32

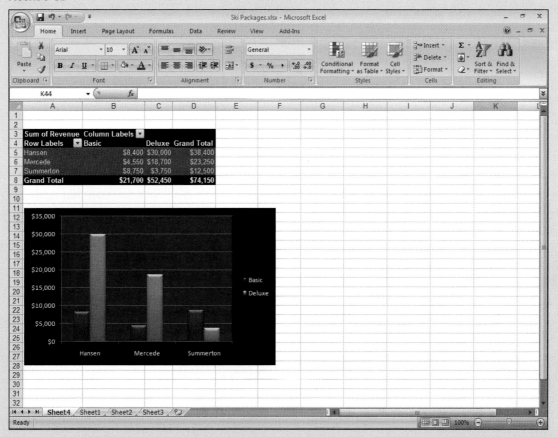

Upgrading to Access 2007

After you upgrade to Microsoft Office Access 2007, you will notice its new features as soon as you start the program. Microsoft redesigned the Access window so you can navigate a database with confidence and easily keep track of open windows and objects. Users new to databases can appreciate the professionally designed templates for databases, tables, and fields in Access 2007. Experienced database developers can use advanced tools for quickly creating and adapting database applications to changing business needs. All users can appreciate the innovative Layout View for designing forms and reports with actual data that shows exactly how the form or report will appear when displayed or printed. In this unit, you will explore the major new features of Access 2007, performing typical tasks so you can start working productively.

OBJECTIVES

Access 2007 overview: What's new?

Learn new ways to perform typical tasks

Learn new ways to create tables

Learn new data-entry tools

Learn new query features

Learn new types of forms and views

Learn new ways to design reports

Learn new database management features

Learn other new features

Access 2007 Overview: What's New?

Microsoft Office Access 2007 represents a significant upgrade over earlier releases of Access, with improvements that let you quickly track, report, and share information in a secure, manageable program. If you are new to database design, Access 2007 provides innovative, interactive ways to design tables, forms, and reports. Access 2007 includes a library of professionally designed templates for databases, tables, and fields so you can create useful, appealing databases as soon as you start the program. If you are an experienced database designer, you'll appreciate the enhanced features for working with data from many sources, including Microsoft SQL Server, and distributing data using SharePoint services and expanded export options. The first change you'll notice, however, is the redesigned window, which replaces menus and toolbars with a streamlined Ribbon. 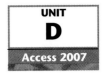 In this lesson, you will get acquainted with some of the new Access features.

DETAILS

As you begin to explore Access 2007, look for changes in the following areas:

- **New ways to get started**

  When you start Access 2007, the Getting Started with Microsoft Office Access page opens, providing database templates you can use immediately to store and track your data. You can also enhance and refine these templates to suit your needs. If you start with a blank database, Access 2007 lets you create a table in Datasheet View so you can see how the table will look to users as you are designing it.

- **New ways to perform database tasks**

  Instead of menus and toolbars, you now work with a streamlined Ribbon to perform tasks. Each tab on the Ribbon organizes buttons into logical groups so you can quickly find familiar features and try new ones. Tables, queries, forms, and reports also open as tabbed documents in the main window so you can keep track of your open objects. Figure D-1 compares the Access 2003 and 2007 windows.

- **Improved navigation**

  The new Navigation Pane replaces the database window and provides easy access to all of your database objects. In the Navigation Pane, you can organize your objects by type or date modified, for example, and view them with details, as icons, or in a list. To allow yourself plenty of work space when designing forms and reports, you can collapse the Navigation Pane so it takes up less room, but still remains available. The Access 2007 window in Figure D-1 displays the Navigation Pane.

- **New view for designing forms and reports**

  The new Layout View lets you make design changes to forms and reports while you display data. For example, you can add, remove, and rearrange fields, apply an AutoFormat from an updated set of designs, and change the properties of controls. Figure D-2 shows a form and report in Layout View.

- **Professional-looking AutoFormats**

  Access 2007 lets you choose from a new set of AutoFormats, which are more sophisticated than those offered in earlier versions. You can use an AutoFormat as it is, or you can customize it to fit your preferences by changing colors or adding graphics. The form and report in Figure D-2 use the new Civic AutoFormat.

- **New types of forms and data types**

  Use the new split form to create a form that combines a Datasheet View in one part of the window and a Form View in another part. You specify whether to place the datasheet on the top, bottom, left, or right of the window. Figure D-3 shows the datasheet below the Form View. Access 2007 also provides two new data types for fields: Attachment and multivalued. A multivalued field can store more than one value, such as two employee names or a list of products. An Attachment field can store files such as graphics and text documents.

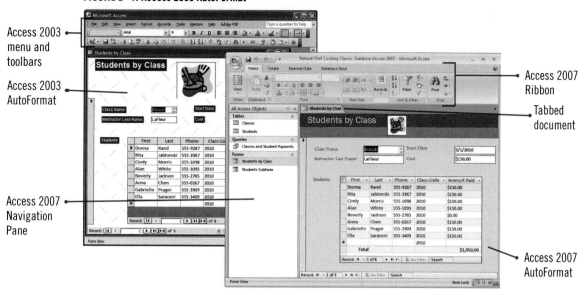

FIGURE D-1: Access 2003 AutoFormat

Access 2003 menu and toolbars

Access 2003 AutoFormat

Access 2007 Navigation Pane

Access 2007 Ribbon

Tabbed document

Access 2007 AutoFormat

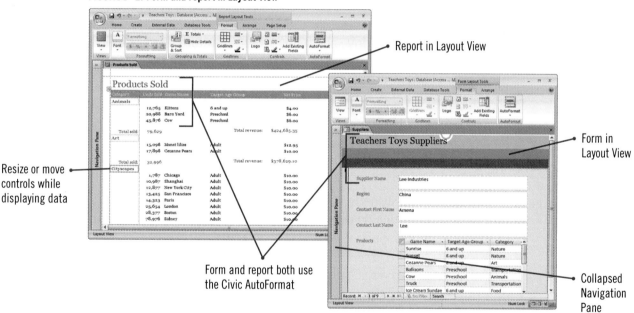

FIGURE D-2: Form and report in Layout View

Resize or move controls while displaying data

Report in Layout View

Form in Layout View

Collapsed Navigation Pane

Form and report both use the Civic AutoFormat

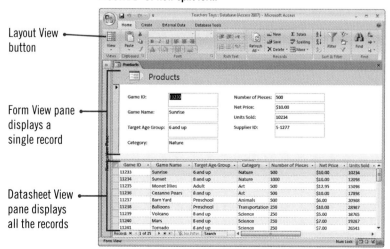

FIGURE D-3: New split form

Layout View button

Form View pane displays a single record

Datasheet View pane displays all the records

Learning New Ways to Perform Typical Tasks

When you first start Access 2007, the new Getting Started with Microsoft Office Access page appears, listing professionally designed database templates and options for creating and opening databases. Instead of using the database window and Objects bar, as you did in Access 2003, you select objects from the Navigation Pane, which remains open on the left side of the Access window. When you open an object, it appears on a tab in the main Access window so you can easily keep track of objects. Like other Office 2007 programs, instead of toolbars and menus, Access 2007 includes a Ribbon that organizes tools logically and in context so you can quickly find the ones you need. ▓▓▓▓▓ In this lesson, you will explore the Access 2007 main window and navigate objects.

STEPS

1. **Start Access**

   The Getting Started with Microsoft Office Access page opens, shown in Figure D-4. You use this window to find online resources and to create or open a database, including a database based on a template.

TROUBLE
If you have not opened the Contacts template before, Access prepares it for first time use.

2. **In the Template Categories list, click** Local Templates, **click** Contacts, **click the** Browse icon 🗁, **navigate to the drive and folder where you store your Data Files, click** OK, **then click** Create

   The Contacts database opens and displays the Contact List form and a Security Warning, which you can close.

3. **Click the** Options button **on the Security Warning bar, click** Enable this content, **click** OK, **then click the** Shutter Bar Open/Close button 》

   The Navigation Pane is organized to display only forms and reports related to the Contacts table, as shown in Figure D-5, but you can change that organization to display all the objects or to group them logically by a different characteristic, such as by object type.

4. **Click the** Contacts Navigation bar **in the Navigation Pane, click** Object Type, **double-click the** Contacts **table, double-click the** Contacts Extended **query, then double-click the** Contact Phone List **report**

   When you open an object, it appears as a **tabbed document** in the main part of the Access window. You click a document tab to switch from one object to another. Next, you can explore the Ribbon.

5. **Click the** Create tab **on the Ribbon, review its tools, click the** External Data tab, **click the** Database Tools tab, **then click the** Home tab

   Table D-1 describes the tools on each tab and the location of that tab's commands in Access 2003.

TROUBLE
If the report does not open in Layout View, click the View button arrow, and then click Layout View.

6. **Click the** View button **in the Views group**

   The Contact Phone List report appears in **Layout View**, a new view that lets you change the report layout and other design elements while displaying data, if your report includes any. You can change the appearance of a report or form by applying an AutoFormat.

QUICK TIP
To change text characteristics, select the text, then click a button in the Font group on the Report Layout Tools Format tab.

7. **Click the** Report Layout Tools Format tab **if necessary, click the** AutoFormat button **in the** AutoFormat group, **then click** Opulent **(fourth row, second from left)**

   The Opulent AutoFormat displays a gradient purple background for the light report title and field names. You are finished with the Contacts database, so you can close it.

8. **Click the** Office button 🗔, **click** Close Database, **then click** Yes **to save your changes**

FIGURE D-4: Getting Started wtih Microsoft Office Access page

Local Templates link

Categories of templates available online

Featured online templates

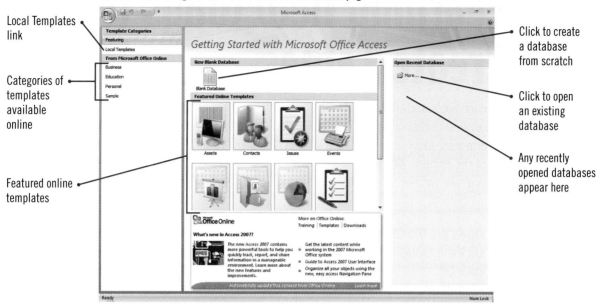

Click to create a database from scratch

Click to open an existing database

Any recently opened databases appear here

FIGURE D-5: Contact List form open in the Contacts database

Navigation Pane title bar

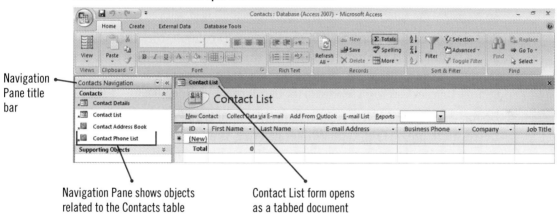

Navigation Pane shows objects related to the Contacts table

Contact List form opens as a tabbed document

TABLE D-1: Access tab summary

tab name	contains information relating to	contains these groups	Office 2003 menu locations
Home	The most commonly used commands in Access	Views, Clipboard, Font, Rich Text, Records, Sort & Filter, Find	Edit, View, Records
Create	Creating tables, forms, reports, and queries	Tables, Forms, Reports, Other	File
External Data	Importing from and exporting to other data sources	Import, Export, Collect Data, SharePoint Lists	Tools
Database Tools	Automating, analyzing, and managing the database	Macro, Show/Hide, Analyze, Move Data, Database Tools	Tools

Learning New Ways to Create Tables

Although you could create a table in Access 2003 by entering data in Datasheet View, you had to use Table Design View to change field names, assign data types, and specify the primary key. In Access 2007, you can perform these tasks while creating a table in Datasheet View. To do so, you use the tools on the Datasheet tab of the Ribbon.  In this lesson, you will open the Outdoors database, which contains data for tracking sales for a wholesaler of recreational supplies, then use Datasheet View to create a table of products.

STEPS

1. **Open the file Outdoors.accdb from the drive and folder where you store your Data Files, click the Options button on the Security Warning bar, click Enable this content, then click OK**

   Access 2007 has a new file format, which uses the file extension .accdb. The Outdoors database opens, displaying its objects in the Navigation Pane.

> **QUICK TIP**
>
> When you create a blank database, you start working with an empty table named Table1 in Datasheet View.

2. **Click the Create tab, then click the Table button in the Tables group**

   An empty table named Table1 opens in the main Access window, which includes a primary key field named ID and a column labeled "Add New Field" where you create the first new field for the table. See Figure D-6. You want to change the name of the ID field.

3. **Right-click the ID column heading, click Rename Column, then type Product ID**

   Access assigns the AutoNumber data type to the default ID field, but you can change it if necessary.

4. **Press [↓] to select the first field in the Product ID column, click the Data Type list arrow in the Data Type & Formatting group on the Datasheet tab, then click Text**

   The data type for the Product ID field changes from AutoNumber to Text. Because this is the primary key field, the Unique check box is selected in the Data Type & Formatting group.

> **QUICK TIP**
>
> As you type field names, Access displays them in italics, indicating that they are new names.

5. **Double-click the Add New Field column heading, type Product Type, press [Tab], type Description, press [Tab], type Wholesale Price, then press [Tab]**

   Access assigns the Text data type to each new field. You can change the data type with the Data Type list arrow or by entering data and letting Access detect the type. First, you need to resize the Wholesale Price column.

6. **Point to the right edge of the Wholesale Price field until the pointer changes to ↔, then double-click**

   The column resizes to its best fit, which displays the entire field name text. Now you can enter the first record of product data.

> **QUICK TIP**
>
> If you enter a numeric value with a dollar sign and comma, as in $11,599, Access assigns the Currency data type to that field.

7. **Click in the first row for the Product ID field, type B1003, press [Tab], type Boat, press [Tab], type Laser sailboat, press [Tab], type 11599, press [Tab], resize the Product Type column to its best fit, then click in the first row of the Wholesale Price column**

   The new record is shown in Figure D-7. Access assigns the Number data type to the Wholesale Price column, but you can change it to the Currency data type by applying the Currency format.

8. **Click the Apply Currency Format button $ in the Data Type & Formatting group**

   You can use a field template to add a field for the product manufacturer to the new table.

9. **Click the New Field button in the Fields & Columns group, double-click Manufacturer in the Field Templates pane, click in the first row of the Manufacturer column, type Northeast Boating, press [Enter], then close the Field Templates pane**

   Now you can save the table and give it a descriptive name.

10. **Click the Save button 🖫 on the Quick Access toolbar, type Products, then click OK**

FIGURE D-6: Creating a table in Datasheet View

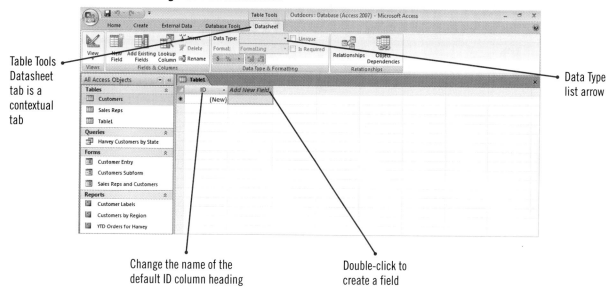

Table Tools Datasheet tab is a contextual tab

Data Type list arrow

Change the name of the default ID column heading

Double-click to create a field

FIGURE D-7: Adding a record and changing a data type

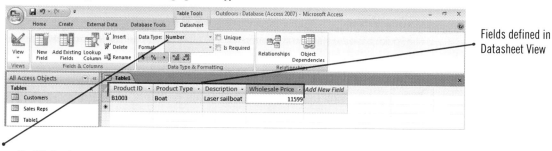

Fields defined in Datasheet View

When you change the Wholesale Price value, Access assigns the Number data type to that field

Saving objects and databases

You use the Save button on the Quick Access toolbar to save the design of the active object. If you are creating a table, for example, click the Save button to save the table design. As you enter or change the data in the table, Access saves it automatically—you don't need to click the Save button. If you want to save an object with a different name or save the entire database using a different name, location, or format, click the Office button and then point to Save As to display the Save As options, shown in Figure D-8. Select Save Object As to save the current object as a new object in the database. Select an option in the "Save the database in another format" section to choose a name and location for saving the entire database using the specified Access file format.

FIGURE D-8: Save As commands

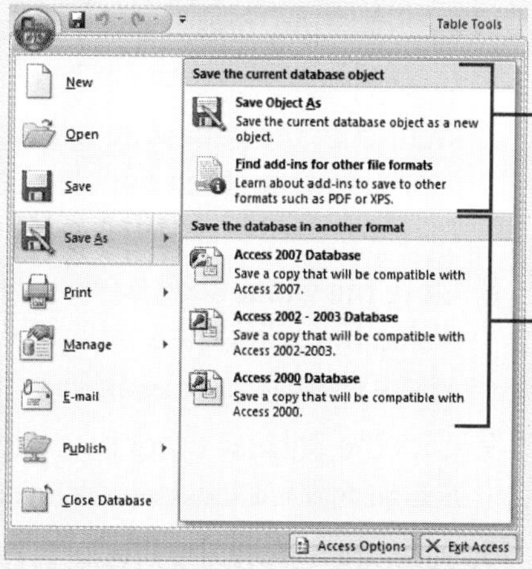

"Save the current database object" section

"Save the database in another format" section

Learning new Data-entry Tools

As in Access 2003, Access 2007 offers more than one way to enter data in a table. Besides entering records directly into a table or form, you can copy records from another table that has the same design, import data from an Excel worksheet, another Access database, or a text file. Access 2007 now features **Attachment fields**, which let you add one or more files to a record, and **multivalued fields**, which you use to store and then select more than one value in a field. ▄▄▄▄ In this lesson, you will add an Attachment field and a multivalued field to the Products table.

STEPS

1. **Click the View button in the Views group on the Table Tools Datasheet tab to open the Products table in Design View**

2. **Click the first blank row in the Field Name column, type Photos, press [Tab], click the Data Type list arrow, then click Attachment**

   You can only create Attachment fields in databases you save in the Access 2007 file format with an .accdb file extension.

3. **Press [Tab] twice, type Sold By, press [Tab], click the Data Type list arrow, then click Lookup Wizard**

   The Lookup Wizard starts so you can select the table and its values, then specify that you want to allow multiple values in the field. The most common type of multivalued field is one that displays values stored in another table in the database.

4. **Click Next to look up the values in a table or query, click Table: Sales Reps, click Next, click Rep Last Name, click the Select Single Field button > , click Next, click Next without specifying a sort field, click Next to accept the list of sales rep names, click the Allow Multiple Values check box, click Finish, then click Yes to save the table**

   Selecting the Allow Multiple Values check box makes the Sold By field a multivalued field. Otherwise, it would be a standard Lookup field.

5. **Click the View button in the Views group to display the Products table in Datasheet View**

   The Attachment field appears with a paper clip icon as its field name even though you specified Photos as the name. Each record also includes a paper clip icon with the number of files attached to the field in parentheses. See Figure D-9.

6. **Double-click the paper clip icon for the first record, click Add in the Attachments dialog box, navigate to the drive and folder where you store your Data Files, click Sailboat1.jpg, press [Shift], click Sailboat2.jpg, release [Shift], click Open, then click OK**

   The two photo files are now included with the first record.

7. **Right-click the paper clip icon for the first record, click Manage Attachments on the shortcut menu, then double-click Sailboat1.jpg to open it**

   The photo opens in the default graphics viewer on your computer, such as Windows Photo Gallery.

8. **Close the window displaying the Sailboat1.jpg image, click Cancel in the Attachments dialog box, click the Sold By field for the first record, then click the Sold By list arrow**

   A list of sales reps opens, as shown in Figure D-10. You can select more than one sales rep in the Sold By field.

9. **Click the Solanas check box, click the Rhodes check box, then click OK**

   Both Solanas and Rhodes appear in the Sold By field for the first record.

10. **Save, then close the Products table**

FIGURE D-9: Products table in Datasheet View

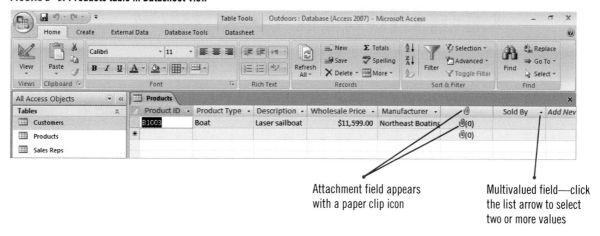

Attachment field appears
with a paper clip icon

Multivalued field—click
the list arrow to select
two or more values

FIGURE D-10: Using a multivalued field

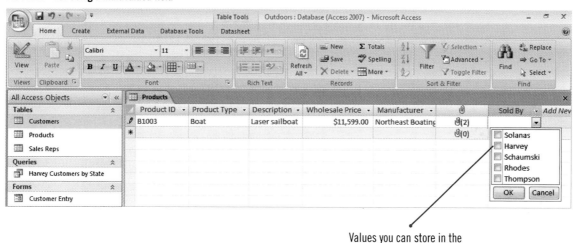

Values you can store in the
Sold By multivalued field

Attaching files to your records

You can use Attachment fields to store more than one file or file type in a field, such as a text document containing a product description and an image file containing a photo of the product. This new data type stores data more efficiently than the earlier Object Linking and Embedding (OLE) technology. In Access 2003, when you used OLE to store images in a record, Access converted the image to a bitmap and embedded it in a record, which usually increased the size of the database file significantly. When you attach a file to a record, it opens in its native program—the one used to create the file—and retains its original format, which keeps the file size low.

Learning New Query Features

Using Access 2007, you can create all the same types of queries you created in Access 2003, including select queries, crosstab queries, and summary queries. Access 2007, however, offers many improvements that help you interpret and analyze the query results. The process of building a crosstab query has been streamlined, whether you use a wizard or Query Design View. You can also include a **Total row** in the query datasheet to display the results of a calculation, and use **AutoFilter** to sort and filter records. ▰▰▰ In this lesson, you decide to create a couple of queries in the Outdoors database to explore the new query features.

STEPS

1. **Double-click the** Customers by Rep **query in the Navigation Pane, change** Vera **in the Rep First Name field to your first name, then change** Solanas **in the Rep Last Name field to your last name**

> **QUICK TIP**
> You can use AutoFilter with any datasheet, including table datasheets.

2. **Click the** Rep Last Name **list arrow**
   An AutoFilter menu opens with options for sorting and filtering field values. See Figure D-11. You want to examine all of Ruth Schaumski's sales.

3. **Click the** (Select All) **check box to clear the selection, click the** Schaumski **check box, then click** OK
   Access filters the datasheet to display only those records where Ruth Schaumski is the sales rep. Now you can display the total amount of her sales this year.

> **QUICK TIP**
> You can also perform other calculations, such as displaying the average, maximum, or minimum value in a field.

4. **Click any** YTD Orders **field, click the** Totals **button in the Records group, click the** YTD Orders **field in the Total row, click the** list arrow**, click** Sum**, if necessary, then press** [↑]
   Access adds all the values in the YTD Orders field and displays the total in the Total row for that field. See Figure D-12. Next, you can create a crosstab query that compares the total sales for each sales rep by modifying the Customers by Rep query.

5. **Save and close the query, click the** Create **tab, click the** Query Design **button in the Other group, double-click** Customers**, double-click** Sales Reps**, then click** Close

6. **Double-click the** Customer**,** YTD Orders**, and** Rep Last Name **fields**
   Now you can change this select query into a crosstab query.

7. **Click the** Crosstab **button in the Query Type group, click the right side of the** Crosstab **cell for the Customer field, click** Row Heading**, press** [Tab]**, click the** list arrow **in the Crosstab cell for YTD Orders, click** Value**, click the right side of the** Crosstab **cell for Rep Last Name, click** Column Heading**, click** Group By **for YTD Orders, click the** list arrow**, then click** Sum
   Your query design grid should look like the one in Figure D-13.

8. **Click the** View **button in the Results group on the Query Tools Design tab**
   The crosstab datasheet summarizes the 64 sales records by showing the total amount of sales each rep generated from each customer.

9. **Save the query as** Sales Crosstab**, click the** Office button **⊕, point to** Print**, click** Print Preview**, click** Landscape **in the Page Layout group, print the first page of the datasheet, click the** Close Print Preview button **in the Close Preview group, then close the query**

FIGURE D-11: Using AutoFilter to filter a datasheet

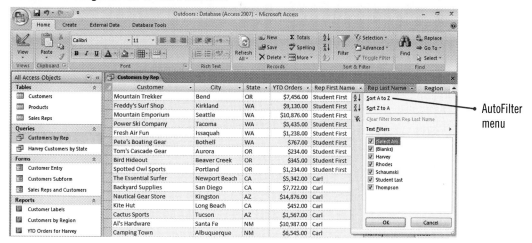

AutoFilter menu

FIGURE D-12: Including a Total row

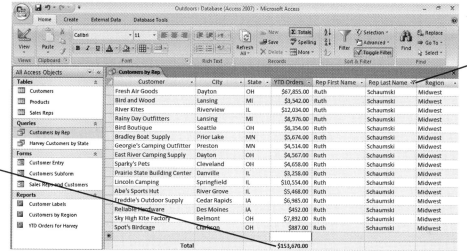

Datasheet is filtered to show only Ruth Schaumski's orders

Total row calculates the total year-to-date sales

FIGURE D-13: Designing a crosstab query

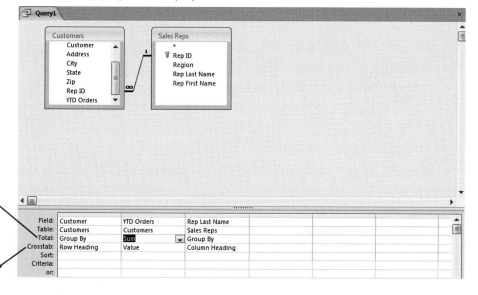

Use the Total row to select a calculation for the Value field

Use the Crosstab row to specify how to arrange the fields

Learning new Types of Forms and Uiews

As you already know, one of the major innovations in Access 2007 is Layout View for forms and reports. In **Layout View**, you can modify the form's layout and other design elements while displaying the form data, making it easy to see the results of your design changes. Access 2007 also includes **split forms**, which provides two views of your data at the same time—a Form View on top and a Datasheet View below it. ▓▓▓▓ In this lesson, you will start by creating a split form for the Customers table, then creating a form for the Products table and modifying it in Layout View.

STEPS

QUICK TIP
Use a split form to search for a record in the Datasheet View pane, then edit it in the Form View pane.

1. **Click the Customers table in the Navigation Pane, click the Create tab, then click the Split Form button in the Forms group**

   The new Customers form opens in Layout View, as shown in Figure D-14. The top Form View pane shows one record at a time, while the bottom Datasheet View pane displays many records. You want to edit the record for Woodstock Outdoor Gear.

QUICK TIP
To remove a sort from a field, click the Clear All Sorts button 🔁 in the Sort & Filter group.

2. **Click the View button in the Views group to switch to Form View, click the Customer list arrow in the Datasheet View pane, then click Sort Z to A**

   You can use the AutoFilter feature to sort records in ascending or descending order. The Woodstock Outdoor Gear record appears at the top of the datasheet and in the Form View pane.

3. **In the Form View pane, change the address to 53 Pine Street, then press [Enter]**

   The address also changes in the datasheet.

TROUBLE
If the Products form opens in Form View, click the View button in the Views group to switch to Layout View.

4. **Save the form as Customers, close the form, click the Products table in the Navigation Pane, click the Create tab, then click the Form button in the Forms group**

   The new Products form opens in Layout View.

5. **Click the Shutter Bar Open/Close button ≪ to close the Navigation Pane**

   You decide to resize the fields so they take up less space on the form.

6. **Click B1003 (the Product ID field value) to select the field if necessary, point to the right edge of the orange selection box until the pointer changes to a resize pointer ↔, then drag to the left so the fields are about half as wide**

   The Products form in Layout View should look like Figure D-15. Next, you can explore some new design shortcuts available in Layout View.

7. **Click the Title button in the Controls group to select the form title, click the Line Type button ▦ ▾ in the Controls group, then click Solid**

   The Products title now appears with a solid outline.

8. **Click the Date and Time button in the Controls group, then click OK**

   The current date and time appear to the right of the form title.

9. **Save the form as Products, then close it**

Turning a form into a split form

You can turn any form into a split form. Good candidates are forms that include many records but not too many fields so you can see all the fields in the Form View and Datasheet View panes. To modify a form so it becomes a split form, open the form in Design View, open the Property Sheet for the form, click the Format tab, click the Default View list arrow, then click Split Form. When the split form is open in Design View, you can set other split form properties in the Property Sheet, such as whether the datasheet appears above, below, to the left, or to the right of the form, and whether you want to freeze the position of the splitter bar. See Figure D-16.

FIGURE D-14: Customers split form in Layout view

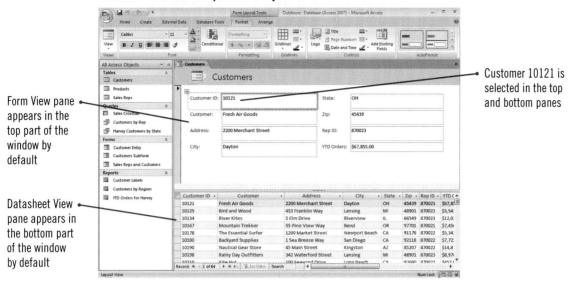

Form View pane appears in the top part of the window by default

Customer 10121 is selected in the top and bottom panes

Datasheet View pane appears in the bottom part of the window by default

FIGURE D-15: Products form in Layout View

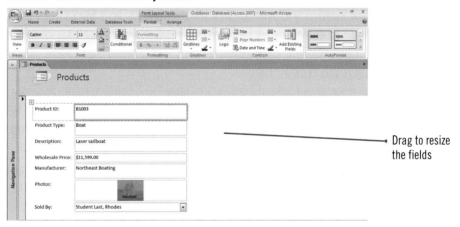

Drag to resize the fields

FIGURE D-16: Turning a form into a split form

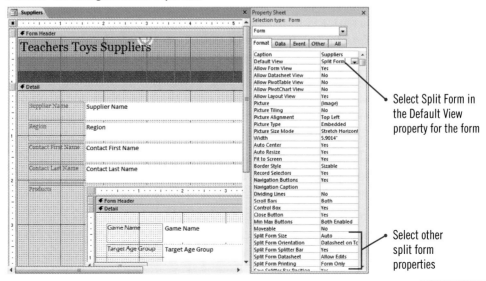

Select Split Form in the Default View property for the form

Select other split form properties

Learning New Ways to Design Reports

As with forms, you can modify a report in Layout View to change its design while displaying data. This is especially useful when creating reports because you usually need to make sure all the report fields fit on a sheet of paper in portrait or landscape view. You can use the new **Group, Sort, and Total pane** to organize records in a report. In this lesson, you will create a report showing the customers for each sales rep, then modify the report in Layout View.

STEPS

1. **Click the** Shutter Bar Open/Close button ⧉ **to open the Navigation Pane, click the** Customers by Rep **query, click the** Create tab, **then click the** Report Wizard button **in the** Reports group

   The first Report Wizard dialog box opens so you can select the fields for the report.

2. **Click the** Select All Fields button ⧉, **click** Next, **click** by Sales Reps, **click** Next, **double-click** State **to add another grouping level, then click** Next

   You also want to include some summary calculations on the report.

3. **Click** Summary Options, **click the** Sum, Min, **and** Max check boxes, **click** OK, **click the** list arrow **to select a sort field, click** YTD Orders, **click** Next, **click** Next **to accept the layout and orientation, click** Module, **click** Next, **enter** Sales Reps and Customers **as the report title, then click** Finish

   The report opens in Print Preview. See Figure D-17. Your screen might display different items, depending on the name you entered earlier. You can improve the layout of the report in Layout View.

   TROUBLE
   If the report doesn't appear in Layout View, click the View button arrow in the Views group, then click Layout View.

4. **Click the** Close Print Preview button **in the Close Preview group**

   You can start formatting the report in Layout View by widening the Customer column.

5. **Click a** Customer **field value, point to the right edge of an orange selection box until the pointer changes to a resize pointer ↔, then drag to the right to display the entire field values, then resize the** Region **field values the same way**

   You may need to scroll down to verify that all Customer names and Regions are fully displayed. Next, you can select the three calculated fields and resize them to display their values.

   QUICK TIP
   You can also use the Form Layout Tools Arrange tab when modifying a form in Layout View.

6. **Click a** Sum **field value (currently displaying ##), press and hold** [Shift], **click a** Min **field value, click a** Max **field value, release** [Shift] **to select the three field values, then drag the left edge of a selection box to display the entire values**

   You can use tools on the Report Layout Tools Arrange tab to align the fields. Table D-2 lists the tools available on the Format and Arrange tabs in Layout View for forms and reports.

   QUICK TIP
   Use the Align Text Left ▤ ,Center ▤ , and Align Text Right ▤ on the Report Layout Tools Format tab to align text within a control.

7. **Click anywhere on the form to remove the selection, select the** Sum, Min, **and** Max **labels, click the** Report Layout Tools Arrange tab, **then click the** Align Right button **in the Control Alignment group to right-align the labels on the report**

   You also want to sort the records for each sales rep so the cities appear in alphabetic order.

8. **Click the** Report Layout Tools Format tab, **click the** Group & Sort button **in the Grouping & Totals group, click** Sort by YTD Orders, **click the** from smallest to largest list arrow, **then click** from largest to smallest

   Figure D-18 shows the redesigned report in Layout View.

9. **Click the** View button arrow **in the Views group, click** Print Preview, **click** Margins **in the Page Layout group, click** Narrow **if necessary, navigate to the page displaying your name in the Rep fields, print that page only, close Print Preview, then save and close the report**

FIGURE D-17: Sales Reps and Customers report

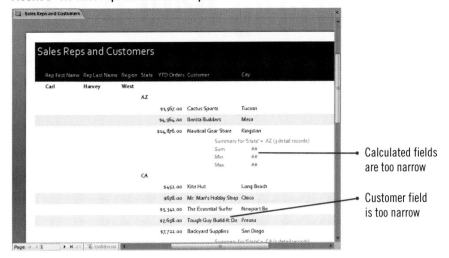

Calculated fields are too narrow

Customer field is too narrow

FIGURE D-18: Redesigning the Sales Reps and Customers form

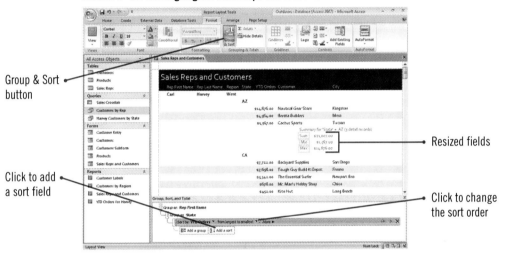

Group & Sort button

Click to add a sort field

Resized fields

Click to change the sort order

TABLE D-2: Tools Available in Layout View for Forms and Reports

tab name	group name	description	forms	reports
Format	Views	Switch to Print Preview (reports only), or to Form, Layout, or Design View	X	X
	Font	Change the font, style, or color of the text or background, and set conditional formatting rules	X	X
	Formatting	Apply a formatting style, such as currency	X	
	Grouping & Totals	Group and sort fields in a report, display totals, and hide details		X
	Gridlines	Display gridlines or set characteristics of lines	X	X
	Controls	Insert controls such as a logo or the date and time, or add existing fields (reports only)	X	X
	AutoFormat	Select an AutoFormat or customize one to create your own	X	X
Arrange	Control Layout	Set the layout and spacing of the fields	X	X
	Control Alignment	Align the left, right, top, or bottom borders of controls	X	X
	Position	Set the position of a control	X	X
	Tools	Open the Property Sheet	X	X
Page Setup	Page Layout	Change settings for printing		X

Learning New Database Management Features

Recall that the Navigation Pane in Access 2007 replaces the database window in Access 2003 as the main area for working with database objects. You can change the organization of objects in the Navigation Pane by displaying them in built-in or custom groups, which can make objects easier to find, especially in large databases. By changing the view, you can display more information about each object, such as the date it was created or modified. You can also use the new Manage options on the Office button menu to back up and compact and repair a database. ▓▓▓▓ In this lesson, you will customize the Navigation Pane and change the view of its objects.

STEPS

QUICK TIP

You can also click the Navigation Pane arrow button ▼ to open the Navigation Pane menu.

1. **At the top of the Navigation Pane, click the** All Access Objects bar

   The Navigation Pane menu opens, shown in Figure D-19. You can change the category used to display options by selecting an option in the Navigate to Category section. You can change the grouping option in the Filter By Group section.

2. **Click** Tables and Related Views, **then click the** Sales Reps bar

   The Navigation Pane now organizes the objects in the database in three groups: those related to the Customers table, Sales Reps table, and Products table. Objects related to more than one table appear in the Navigation Pane more than once. When you click the Sales Reps bar, the Sales Reps group collapses.

3. **Right-click the** All Tables bar, **point to** View By, **then click** Details

   Details about each object appear in the Navigation Pane, including the date it was created and modified.

4. **Drag the** splitter bar **between the Navigation Pane and object area to widen the Navigation Pane by about an inch, right-click the** All Tables bar, **then click** Navigation Options

   The Navigation Options dialog box opens, shown in Figure D-20. You use this dialog box to create custom groups.

QUICK TIP

Be sure you click the Custom Group 1 name and not the check box.

5. **Click** Custom **in the Categories list, click** Custom Group 1 **in the Groups list, click** Rename Group, **type** Mailings, **press [Enter], click the** Add Group button, **type** Management, **then click** OK

   Now you can organize objects in the new groups.

6. **Right-click the** All Tables bar, **point to** Category, **click** Custom, **then scroll to the top of the Navigation Pane, if necessary**

   You reorganize the objects by dragging them to a custom group. When you do, they appear as shortcuts, indicating they are links you can double-click to open the actual object.

7. **Drag the** Harvey Customers by State **query to the** Management **group, scroll down then drag the** Customer Labels **report to the** Mailings **group**

   You can rename a custom group after adding it to the Navigation Pane.

8. **Right-click the** Management bar, **click** Rename, **type** Sales Analysis, **then press [Enter]**

   Figure D-21 shows the customized Navigation Pane.

9. **Close the database, then exit Access**

FIGURE D-19: Changing the view of the Navigation Pane

Navigation
Pane menu

FIGURE D-20: Adding a custom group to the Navigation Pane

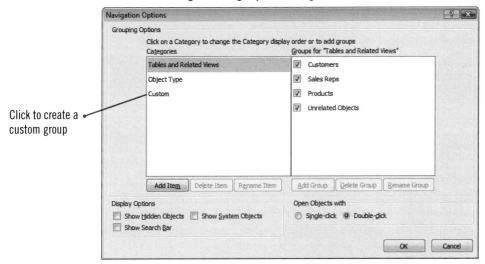

Click to create a
custom group

FIGURE D-21: Adding an object to a custom group

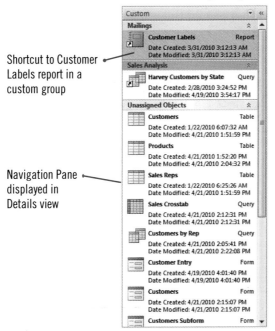

Shortcut to Customer
Labels report in a
custom group

Navigation Pane
displayed in
Details view

Learning Other New Features

Access 2007 includes other upgrades, many of which help you create forms and reports and share data with others. Access 2007 also provides additional security features, which often work behind the scenes to protect your data. ▧▧▧ In this lesson, you will review some other new features of Access 2007.

As you use Access 2007, note these additional features:

- **Stacked and tabular layouts for forms and reports**

  Forms and reports often contain information in tables and columns, such as a column of customer data. When you work in Layout or Design View for a form or report, use the Tabular and Stacked buttons in the Control Layout group on the Arrange tab to group controls so you can manipulate them as a unit. See Figure D-22.

- **Improved field list for adding fields to forms and reports**

  Figure D-22 also shows an expanded field list, which includes fields from all the tables in your database, letting you drag fields to a form or report even if they are stored in an unrelated table. If necessary, Access 2007 guides you through the steps of defining a relationship so you can add a field to an object.

- **Alternate background color**

  You can display an alternating background color in datasheets, reports, and continuous forms, which shades every other line of data. Using an alternate background color is especially helpful when you display a Total row in a datasheet. See Figure D-23.

- **Calendar for selecting dates**

  When you are entering dates in a datasheet or form, a calendar icon ▦ appears next to date fields so you can select dates from a monthly calendar. Figure D-23 also shows a calendar for a date field.

- **Export to PDF and XML**

  To enhance printing and distributing your Access data, you can export data to a Portable Document Format (PDF) or XML Paper Specification (XPS) format. To do so, you need to install the Publish as a PDF or XPS add-in, which is available as a program you can download from the Microsoft Web site. When you export a form, report, or datasheet to a PDF or XPS file, you preserve your formatting and layout without requiring others to have Access installed on their computers to print or review your output.

- **Embedded macros**

  Access 2007 lets you associate a macro with a control by embedding it in a control's event property, such as one for a button. Users can then click the button to open a form or report—you no longer need to use VBA code to accomplish this task.

- **Enhanced security**

  The Access 2007 security features help to protect your data and maintain consistency with other Office 2007 programs. You can open an Access 2007 database that contains trusted programming code or macros, confident that others have not tampered with that code. You can also disable the code or macros before distributing the database to others.

- **SharePoint services**

  To share and manage data, use Access 2007 with Microsoft Windows SharePoint Services 3.0. Move or publish Access data on a SharePoint Web site so you can collaborate with others in your organization. You can store information in lists on a SharePoint Web site, then access the data through linked tables in an Access database, or you can store the entire Access file on the SharePoint Web site. If you administer a database, you can track versions of data, subscribe to alerts so that you know when changes are made, and manage permissions for the data.

- **What's gone**

  With all the new Access 2007 features, it was inevitable that other features would be discontinued. In addition to replacing OLE technology, Microsoft also retired data access pages.

FIGURE D-22: Improvements for working with forms and reports

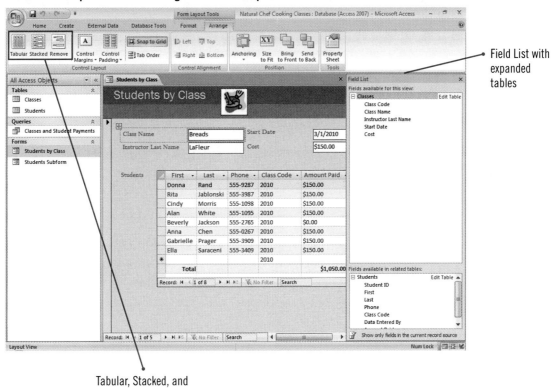

Field List with expanded tables

Tabular, Stacked, and Remove buttons

FIGURE D-23: Datasheet improvements

Alternate Fill/Back color

Calendar icon for selecting dates in a Date/Time field

Choosing a file format

Recall that Access 2007 introduces a new file format that uses the .accdb file extension, not the .mdb extension. Although you can open .mdb databases in Access 2007, Microsoft recommends that you save them using the new file format so you can take advantage of new features such as multivalued fields and attachments. (These features are available only in .accdb databases.) Keep in mind that you cannot link or open databases with the new file format in earlier versions of Access. Furthermore, if you need to use replication or user-level security, you must use an earlier file format because Access 2007 does not support these features. To convert an .mdb database to the new .accdb file format, open the database in Access 2007, click the Office button, point to Save As, and then click Access 2007 Database.

Practice

▼ CONCEPTS REVIEW

Label each element of the Access window shown in Figure D-24.

FIGURE D-24

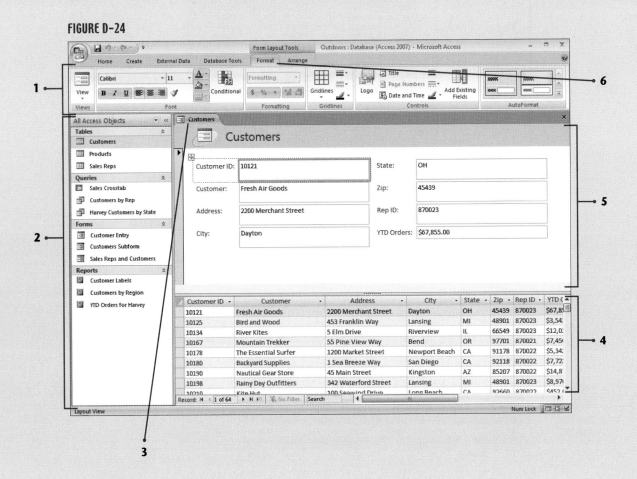

Upgrading to Access 2007

▼ SKILLS REVIEW

1. Learn new ways to perform typical tasks.

  a. Start Access, open a database based on the Assets local template, then save the database as **Assets.accdb** in the drive and folder where you store your Data Files. Enable content as necessary.

  b. Expand the Navigation Pane, open the Contacts table, the Assets Extended query, and the Assets By Category report.

  c. Display the Assets By Category report in Layout View.

  d. Change the AutoFormat of the report to Oriel, then save and close the report.

  e. Open the Asset List form in Layout View, then change its AutoFormat to Oriel. Save and close the form.

  f. In the Contacts table, add a record using your school name as the Company, your last name as Last Name, and your first name as First Name. Leave the other fields blank, then close the Contacts table.

  g. Close the Assets database.

2. Learn new ways to create tables.

  a. Open the file Bicycles.accdb from the drive and folder where you store your Data Files, then enable content as necessary.

  b. In Datasheet View, create a table named Suppliers. Rename the default ID field to **Supplier ID**. Make sure it uses the AutoNumber data type.

  c. Add three fields to the table: **Company Name**, **Product Type**, and **Discount Offered**.

  d. Enter the two records shown in Table D-3, pressing [Tab] in the Supplier ID field to accept the number Access automatically assigns.

  e. Resize the columns to their best fit, then change the data type of the Discount Offered field to Yes/No, if necessary. (Click Yes if a message appears about losing data.)

  f. Use the Field Templates pane to add a new field to the table based on the Acquired Date field in the Assets table. Change the name of the new field to **First Contact**.

  g. In the First Contact field for the first record, enter **5/15/2009**. For the second record, enter **2/12/2010**.

  h. Save the table, naming it **Suppliers**.

TABLE D-3

Supplier ID	Company Name	Product Type	Discount Offered
(auto)	Channing Cycles	Mountain bikes	No
(auto)	your name	Specialty bikes	Yes

3. Learn new data-entry tools.

  a. Switch to Design View of the Suppliers table.

  b. Enter a new field named **Pictures** and assign the Attachment data type to it.

  c. Enter another new field named **Employee Contacts**, then use the Lookup Wizard to display multiple values from the Last Name field in the Employees table in the new field. (*Hint*: Be sure to select the Allow Multiple Values check box to make this a multivalued field.)

  d. Save the table, then switch to Datasheet View. In the Attachments field for Channing Cycles, attach the **Bike.jpg** file from the drive and folder where you store your Data Files.

  e. In the Employee Contacts field for Channing Cycles, select Flanders and Woodruff.

  f. Resize the columns to their best fit, then close the Suppliers table, saving your changes.

4. Learn new query features.

    a. Open the Employee Payroll query, then change Laurel Flanders' name to your name.

    b. Filter the datasheet to display full-time employees only.

    c. Add a Total row to the datasheet that displays the total amount of salary paid to full-time employees. Resize the columns in the datasheet to their best fit, then save and close the query.

    d. Create a query based on the Employees table. Include the Last Name, Dept, and Salary fields in the query.

    e. Switch to Design View, then convert the query to a crosstab query. Select Row Heading for the Last Name field, Column Heading for the Dept field, and Value for the Salary field. Group the Salary field by Sum.

    f. View the query results, save the query as **Employee Crosstab**, print the datasheet, then close the query.

5. Learn new types of forms and views.

    a. Create a split form based on the Employees table. Sort the records in ascending order based on employee last name.

    b. Save the split form as Employees, then close it.

    c. Use the Form tool to create a form based on the Suppliers table.

    d. In Layout View, resize fields and labels as necessary to improve the design of the form.

    e. Add a solid outline to the form title and display the date and time in the title area.

    f. Use Figure D-25 as a guide to refine your form, save it as Suppliers, then close the form.

FIGURE D-25

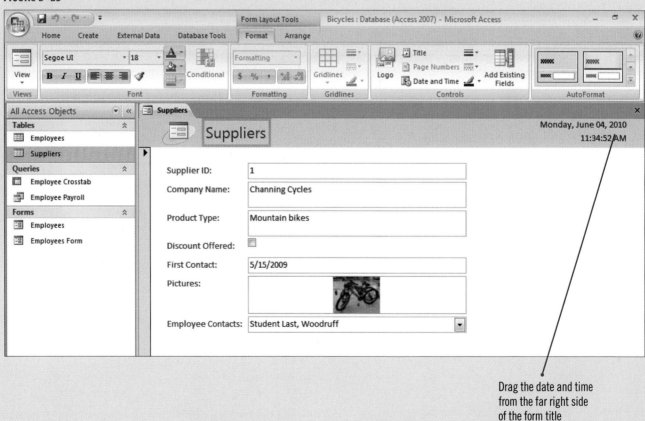

Drag the date and time from the far right side of the form title

6. Learn new ways to design reports.

a. Use the Report Wizard to create a report containing all the fields in the Employee Payroll query. Group the report by Dept, and display the Sum, Min, and Max salary summary calculations.

b. Use a stepped layout, portrait orientation, and Module design. Save the report as **Payroll Analysis**, then examine the report in Print Preview.

c. Switch to Layout View, then resize fields and labels as necessary to display all of the text.

d. In Layout View, move the calculated values for Sum, Min, and Max below the salary values, then right-align those fields with the salary values.

e. Use the Group, Sort, and Total pane to add a sort on Last Name in ascending order.

f. Save the report, then switch to Print Preview. The report should look like Figure D-26.

g. Close the report.

FIGURE D-26

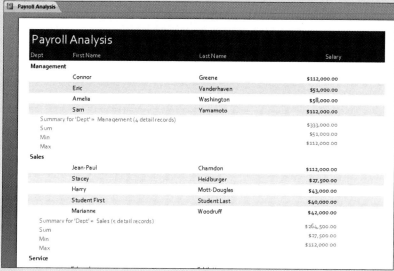

7. Learn new database management features.

a. Change the Navigation Pane to organize the objects in the Bicycles database by Tables and Related Views.

b. View the objects by Icon. Widen the Navigation Pane as necessary.

c. Add a new group named Human Resources to the Navigation Pane.

d. Add the Payroll Analysis report to the Human Resources group.

e. Rename the Human Resources group to **Analysis**. The Navigation Pane should look like Figure D-27.

f. Close the database, then exit Access.

FIGURE D-27

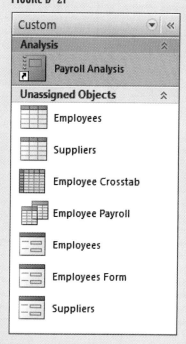

Open the file Games.accdb from the drive and folder where you store your Data Files, then enable content as necessary. Open the Athletes table, then change Stephen James name to your name. Close the table, then use the Report Wizard to create the report shown in Figure D-28, which uses fields from the Athletes, Sponsors, and Charities tables. View the data by Athletes, but do not include any grouping levels. Sort the report by Amount, click the Summary Options button, then sum the amount contributed by each athlete. Select a Stepped layout, Landscape orientation, and the Trek style. Title the report Athlete Contributions. Resize the fields and make other adjustments to match Figure D-28. Print the first page of the report, then save and close it.

FIGURE D-28

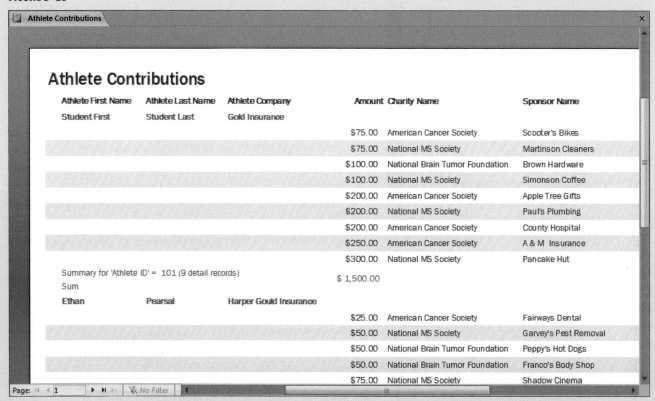

Upgrading to PowerPoint 2007

By upgrading to PowerPoint 2007, you can create presentations that encourage your audience to participate in a visually exciting experience. Best of all, you can create these presentations by keeping the command or tool you want in front of you, instead of searching for it and trying to remember where it is. In PowerPoint 2003, you may have felt the need at times to import graphics created in other programs to achieve a certain look and feel in your presentation. Not so in 2007; you can create and modify impressive charts and diagrams right within the program, and apply effects to shapes, images, and text that communicate your information exactly how you want. In this unit, learn the major new features of PowerPoint 2007 and see how they operate by working with slides in a presentation.

OBJECTIVES

PowerPoint 2007 Overview: What's New?

Learn new ways to perform program tasks

Learn to use new themes and styles

Learn new ways to enhance text and shapes

Learn to create SmartArt graphics

Learn new ways to enhance pictures

Learn new ways to enhance tables and charts

Learn new ways to view handouts

Learn other new features

PowerPoint 2007 Overview: What's New?

PowerPoint 2007 has many new features, along with a new interface to help you use them, and that makes finding and using commands and tools easier and more efficient. 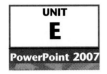 In this lesson, familiarize yourself with the new features in PowerPoint.

In PowerPoint 2007, you will find changes in the following program areas:

- **New ways to perform program tasks**

  The Ribbon replaces menus and toolbars. Figure E-1 compares the opening window of PowerPoint 2003 and 2007. Notice that the main PowerPoint areas, the Slides tab/Outline tab, Slide pane, and Notes pane have not changed; and the View buttons remain on the status bar.

- **New formatting options with themes and styles**

  Your presentation can take on a professional look instantly when you apply a theme and style to it. PowerPoint includes several distinctive themes that coordinate all the elements in a presentation. You can apply different sets of themes, colors, fonts, or effects.

  > **QUICK TIP**
  > You can also apply the same theme to Word documents and Excel spreadsheets.

- **Improved text and shape formatting**

  In PowerPoint 2007 you can choose from an expanded array of WordArt styles fills, and outline styles. You can choose from text effects such as shadows, reflections, glows, 3-D rotation, and transform, which warps text or aligns it on a path.

- **Polished diagrams**

  One of the most dramatic improvements to PowerPoint 2007 is the addition of SmartArt graphics. Using a graphic to present a concept is often the best way to get it across to an audience. With SmartArt, you can choose from several types of diagrams that visually express your idea, such as a timeline, cycle, or list.

- **New ways to enhance pictures and images**

  PowerPoint 2007 has new image-editing tools and features that allow you to adjust the color and pixels in clip art and photographs with precision. You can choose from several preset frame styles, apply a border, or add effects. You can also customize an image by cutting it into a preset shape, such as an arrow or a heart. Figure E-2 shows a slide with an applied theme, SmartArt graphic, and modified clip art image.

  > **QUICK TIP**
  > PowerPoint also includes charting styles and features, such as linking automatically to an Excel spreadsheet.

- **New ways to enhance tables and charts**

  You can choose from many table styles and also apply graphic effects. If you reuse a table created in Word or Excel, PowerPoint preserves the formatting, so it integrates perfectly in the slide.

- **Other new features**

  You can create custom layouts and placeholders, remove hidden data, prevent inadvertent edits, save a presentation as a PDF, and make it compatible with earlier versions of PowerPoint. You can also inspect your presentation in new ways, such as viewing the stacking order of objects on a slide.

FIGURE E-1: Comparing PowerPoint 2003 and 2007

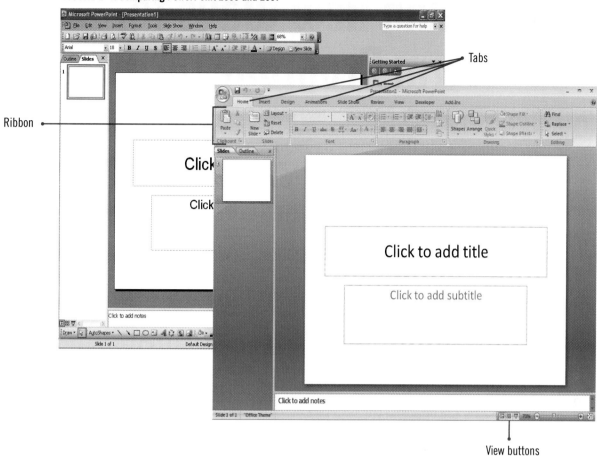

Ribbon

Tabs

View buttons

FIGURE E-2: Viewing a theme and other new features

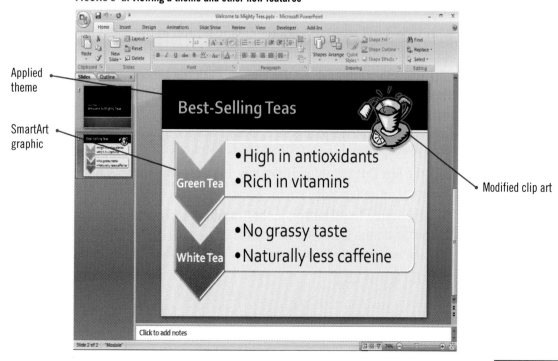

Applied theme

SmartArt graphic

Modified clip art

Learning New Ways to Perform Program Tasks

Across the Office 2007 Suite, the Ribbon creates a visual interface that emphasizes the unique functionality of each application. In PowerPoint 2007, the Ribbon provides top-level access to options that were buried two or more levels deep in PowerPoint 2003, which helps keep your focus on the task at hand. With a little practice, you can acclimate yourself to the new program window fairly quickly. ▰▰▰▰ In this lesson, explore the PowerPoint interface and perform some simple tasks to learn the new landscape.

STEPS

QUICK TIP

You can use most 2003 keyboard short-cuts in PowerPoint 2007, and you can display them by pressing [Alt].

1. **Start PowerPoint**

   The PowerPoint program window opens in Normal view with a new, untitled presentation. By default, PowerPoint opens with the Home tab active. The Home tab contains the commands you use most often. Table E-1 describes the tabs on the Ribbon in PowerPoint.

2. **Open the file E-1.pptx from the drive and folder where you store your Data Files, then save it as Pedal and Paddle Tours**

   The new default file extension in PowerPoint is .pptx; this new format supports XML and results in smaller and more stable files. The presentation contains six slides. All the slide elements are formatted based on the current theme.

3. **Click Slide 2 in the Slides tab, then click the New Slide button in the Slides group on the Ribbon**

   A new title and content slide appear in the Slide pane in the theme of the presentation, as shown in Figure E-3. By default, the New Slide button inserts a Title and Content slide after the currently selected slide. Notice that the command for inserting new slides is on the Home tab, not the Insert tab; that's because inserting a slide is considered a commonly used command.

QUICK TIP

You can immediately insert a different slide layout by click-ing the New Slide button arrow and then clicking a different layout.

4. **Click the Layout button arrow in the Slides group, then click the Title Only layout thumbnail**

   The slide changes to the new layout, which includes only a title placeholder.

5. **Click Slide 2 in the Slides tab, click the New Slide button arrow in the Slides group, then click Duplicate Selected Slides**

   A copy of the selected slide is added to the presentation.

6. **With Slide 3 still selected, click the Delete button in the Slides group**

   The slide is deleted.

QUICK TIP

By default, the Quick Access toolbar includes the Save, Undo, and Redo but-tons; to quickly add a button, right-click a button and then click Add to Quick Access Toolbar; to customize the list or remove buttons, click the Customize Quick Access toolbar button ▼ on the toolbar, then click More Commands.

7. **Click the Animations tab on the Ribbon, click the More button ▼ in the Transition to This Slide group, then point to different transitions in the gallery, but do *not* click the mouse button**

   Each transition is previewed in Slide 3. In most galleries, including Animations, the Live Preview feature shows you what each choice would look like if applied.

8. **Click the Box Out transition (third row, third column under Wipes), as shown in Figure E-4**

   You applied a transition to the selected slide.

9. **Click the Apply To All button in the Transition to This Slide group, then click the Save button 🖫 on the Quick Access toolbar**

   The transition you applied to Slide 3 is applied to all the slides in the presentation.

FIGURE E-3: New slide added to presentation

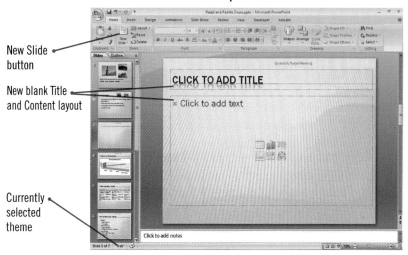

New Slide button

New blank Title and Content layout

Currently selected theme

FIGURE E-4: Viewing the Transitions gallery

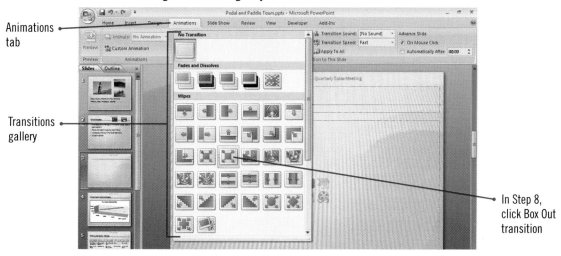

Animations tab

Transitions gallery

In Step 8, click Box Out transition

TABLE E-1: Tabs on the Ribbon in PowerPoint

tab name	contains information relating to	contains these groups	Office 2003 menu
Home	Common tasks in PowerPoint	Clipboard, Slides, Font, Paragraph, Drawing, Editing	Edit, Insert, Format
Insert	Inserting graphics, text, and other media in a slide	Tables, Illustrations, Links, Text, Media Clips	Insert
Design	Page setup, theme designs, colors, fonts, and effects	Page Setup, Themes, Background	File, Format
Animations	Previewing and animating text, slides, graphics, and transitions	Preview, Animations, Transition to This Slide	Slide Show
Slide Show	Viewing slide show, adding narration and timings, monitors	Start Slide Show, Set Up, Monitors	Slide Show
Review	Proofing and collaboration	Proofing, Comments	Insert, Tools
View	Viewing a slideshow, working with masters, displaying workspace	Presentation Views, Show/Hide, Zoom, Color/Grayscale, Window, Macros	View, Tools, Window
Developer	Macros, ActiveX controls	Code, Controls	Tools
Add-Ins	Varies depending on installed products (appears only if add-ins are installed)	Custom Toolbars	Tools

Learning to Use New Themes and Styles

PowerPoint 2007 includes new sophisticated design templates that surpass the formatting and content available in PowerPoint 2003. You can use a template as a starting point and then customize it as you wish. For example, you will usually apply a design theme to your presentation, even if you create it from scratch. **Design themes** apply a distinctive look to the text with bullets, background colors, and graphics. You can easily change the theme or apply a different theme to selected slides. Each theme also has associated **Theme Fonts**, **Theme Colors**, **Theme Effects**, and **Background Styles**. You can often mix and match fonts, colors, and effects without losing the benefit of a coordinated look, although background styles are linked to the selected theme. You can also customize any theme and save it as a unique style in the gallery. Themes are available throughout the Office 2007 suite. In this lesson, select a new design theme and theme color for the presentation, and preview different theme fonts.

STEPS

1. **Click Slide 1 in the Slides tab, click the Design tab on the Ribbon, then point to each theme in the Themes group**

   When you preview a theme, every aspect of the slide design changes with the theme: font size and color, bullets style, backgrounds, page number position, and so on.

> **QUICK TIP**
>
> You can download additional themes by clicking More Themes on Microsoft Office Online at the bottom of the gallery.

2. **Click the More button ▼ in the Themes group, preview additional themes, then click Median (first column, second row under Built-In Themes)**

   The new theme is applied to the presentation giving it a very different appearance, as shown in Figure E-5.

3. **Click the Background Styles button in the Background group, click Style 2, as shown in Figure E-6, then press [Page Down] five times to view the change in each slide**

   The Style 2 background is applied to every slide.

4. **Click the Theme Colors button in the Themes group, then point to several styles to preview them**

   The Theme Colors gallery opens, showing thumbnails of matched color sets, each based on a different theme. The currently selected theme appears on the face of the Theme Colors button.

> **QUICK TIP**
>
> To minimize the Ribbon, double-click a tab name; to maximize it, double-click a tab name again.

5. **Click Trek**

   The Trek theme is applied to the presentation, as shown in Figure E-7. While aspects of the slide design, such as the arrangement of elements and the fonts, do not change, colors do.

6. **Click the Theme Fonts button in the Themes group, then point to several styles to preview them**

   The Themes Font gallery opens, showing thumbnails of heading and body text font pairs.

7. **Click anywhere in the PowerPoint window, then save your changes**

   Because you did not click a new Theme Font, the Median Theme Fonts set is still applied to the presentation.

Using Theme gallery options and customizing themes

When you right-click a theme in the gallery, a shortcut menu of additional options appears. Clicking Apply to Selected Slides applies the theme to certain slides. Clicking Set As Default Theme applies the selected theme to all new presentations and moves the theme to the front of the theme gallery. Clicking Add Gallery to Quick Access Toolbar creates a link to the theme gallery on the Quick Access Toolbar. You can create a custom set of Theme Fonts or Theme Colors by clicking the Create New Theme (Fonts or Colors) command at the bottom of the gallery, selecting the appropriate fonts or colors, and then naming and saving the new theme.

FIGURE E-5: Median theme applied to presentation

Design tab

Median theme

Theme Colors, Theme Fonts, Theme Effects buttons

Background Styles button

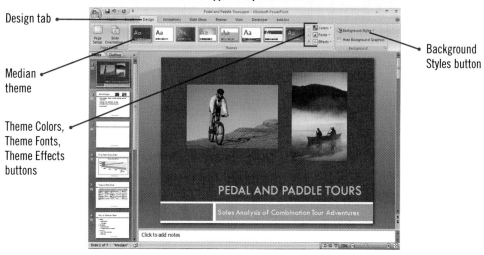

FIGURE E-6: Changing the background style

Background style previewed in slide

Background Styles button

In Step 3, click Style 2

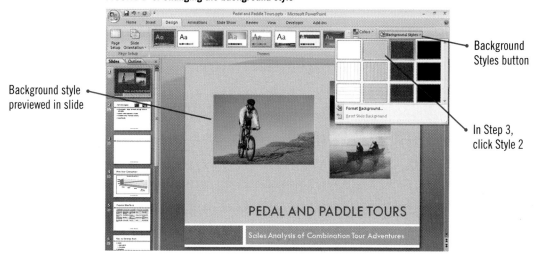

FIGURE E-7: New Theme Colors applied to presentation

Trek Theme Colors

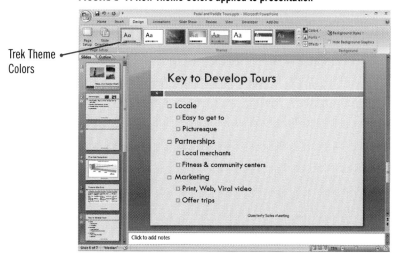

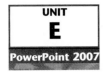

Learning New Ways to Enhance Text and Shapes

In PowerPoint 2003, your ability to work with text was limited to basic formatting options, such as bold and italic, or inserting WordArt. In 2007, there are new fonts, including the new default font, Calibri; other fonts are clearer, have anti-aliasing features, and include OpenType libraries, a type of scalable font. You can modify several attributes, including fill, outline, outline style, shadow, 3-D format, and 3-D rotation for both regular text and WordArt. You can even add columns to a text box. You also have greater control over how a text box fits the amount of text or how the text fits in the text box. ▓▓▓▓ In this lesson, modify text in a text box in the presentation.

STEPS

1. **Move to** Set up more package deals, **Slide 7, select the text** Set up more package deals, **click the** Home tab **on the Ribbon, click the** Bold button **B in the Font group , then click the** Shadow button **S in the Font group**
   The text is now bold and has a shadow effect.

2. **Click the** Clear All Formatting button **in the Font group**
   The formatting is removed from the selected text.

3. **Click the** Increase Font Size button **A in the Font group until** 66 **appears in the Font Size box**
   The text increases in size.

4. **Double-click the** border **around the text until the border is solid**
   The Drawing Tools Format tab opens, as shown in Figure E-8. Remember that in PowerPoint, text is always an object, whether in a placeholder or as part of a graphic. Because of this, in addition to applying regular font formatting options, you can also format text using features in the WordArt Styles group, and format the shape around the text using features in the Shape Styles group.

5. **Click the** More button **in the WordArt Styles group, click the** Fill - Accent 6, Gradient Outline - Accent 6 style **(second column, third row under Applies to Selected Text)**
   The text is has a colored gradient border and shadow applied to it.

6. **Click the** Text Fill button arrow **in the WordArt Styles group, point to several colors, observe changes to the text, then click away from the gallery without making a selection**

7. **Click the** Text Outline button arrow **, point to several choices to preview them, then close the palette**

8. **Click the** Text Effects button **in the WordArt Styles group, point to** Shadow, **then click the** Inside Diagonal Top Left style **(first column, first row under Inner)**
   The text is formatted with a WordArt effect, which gives it depth, as shown in Figure E-9.

9. **Click the** More button **in the Shape Styles group, click the** Intense Effect - Accent 2 style **(third column, sixth row), then save your changes**
   The text box has color and dimension, as shown in Figure E-10.

FIGURE E-8: Drawing Tools Format tab

Drawing Tools Format tab

Text Fill button

Solid text box border

Text Outline button

Text Effects button

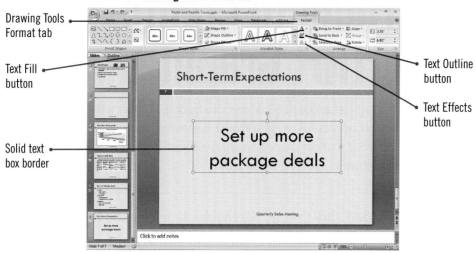

FIGURE E-9: WordArt Style and Text Effect applied to text

WordArt and Text Effect make text stand out from background

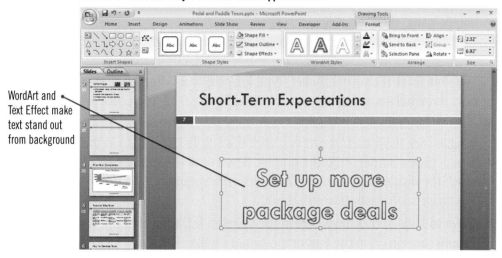

FIGURE E-10: Shape Style applied to text box

Intense Effect — Accent 2 style

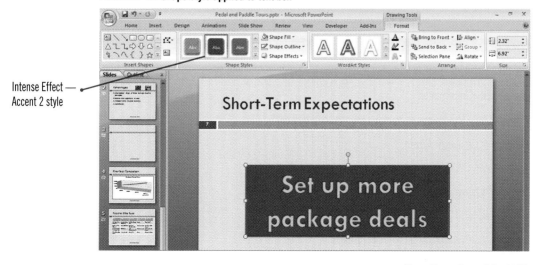

Learning to Create SmartArt Graphics

Although formatted text adequately conveys information, at times a diagram is more effective. SmartArt illustrates information such as organizational hierarchies, processes, and relationships. Layouts are described in Table E-2. You can create a SmartArt diagram from scratch or format existing text.  In this lesson, explore two ways to create SmartArt.

STEPS

1. **Move to Slide 3, click the title placeholder, type Why and How?, then click in the blank area beneath the title you typed**

2. **Click the Insert tab, then click the SmartArt button in the Illustrations group**

   The Choose a SmartArt Graphic dialog box opens, as shown in Figure E-11. The left pane lists the types of layouts, the middle pane shows thumbnails of each, and the right pane shows a preview and description of the current selection.

3. **Click Cycle in the left pane, click Continuous Cycle (first column, second row) in the middle pane, then click OK**

   A blank SmartArt object with the Continuous Cycle layout appears in the slide, with an open text pane, formatted with the current slide theme colors, and the SmartArt Tools Design tab opens on the Ribbon.

4. **Type Fun, click the second bullet, type Friends, type Affordable, Healthy, Family as the next three bullets, compare your screen to Figure E-12, then click away from the SmartArt graphic and text pane**

5. **Double-click the SmartArt graphic, click the Subtle Effect style in the SmartArt Styles group, click a border, drag the graphic down until the top border of "Fun" does not touch the divider bar, then click away from the graphic**

   The graphic has the Subtle Effect style applied.

6. **Move to Slide 6, click anywhere in the bulleted list, then click the Convert to SmartArt Graphic button 🔲 in the Paragraph group on the Home tab**

   A gallery of SmartArt layouts opens.

7. **Click Vertical Bullet List (first column, first row), click the More button in the SmartArt Styles group, click the Polished style (first column, first row under 3-D), click away from the graphic, then save your work**

   The first-level bullets appear three-dimensional with a slick texture, as shown in Figure E-13.

TABLE E-2: SmartArt categories

type	use to show
List	Non-sequential information
Process	Directional flow and connections between parts of a process
Cycle	Repeating or circular processes
Hierarchical	Decision trees, chains of command, and organizational charts
Relationship	Connections between people, objects, or concepts
Matrix	Complex relationships relating to a whole
Pyramid	Proportional or hierarchical sets of relationships

FIGURE E-11: Choose a SmartArt Graphic dialog box

Insert tab

SmartArt button

SmartArt categories

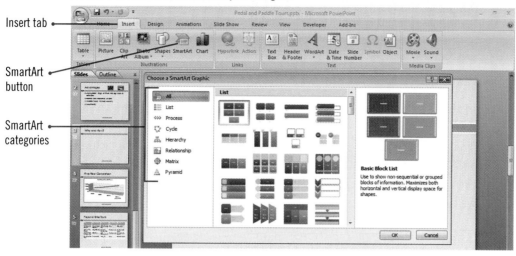

FIGURE E-12: Entering SmartArt text

Text pane

Text pane controls

Continuous Cycle graphic

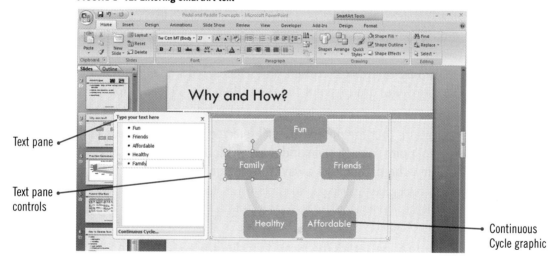

FIGURE E-13: Text converted to SmartArt

Polished SmartArt style

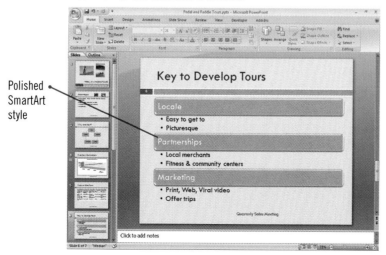

Learning New Ways to Enhance Pictures

PowerPoint 2007 has new tools for adjusting photographs, clip art, and other pictures, including styles for applying a set of adjustments with one mouse click. You can permanently delete pixels in a picture by cropping or removing a color, and you can reduce file size by compressing pictures or adjusting their resolution. PowerPoint offers many picture styles to frame your picture, as well as picture shapes, borders, and effects. ▰▰▱▱▱ In this lesson, add a picture style and effect to some photos in the presentation, and remove color from and add brightness to another photo.

STEPS

1. **Move to Slide 1, press and hold [Shift], click each picture on the slide, then click the Picture Tools Format tab on the Ribbon**

2. **Click the More button ⯆ in the Picture Styles group, point to several styles to preview them, then click the Drop Shadow Rectangle style (fourth column, first row)**

    The style is applied to the photos, resulting in a drop-shadow effect, as shown in Figure E-14. You can further customize pictures using the Picture Shape button, which fits a photo into the shape's contours; the Picture Border button; and the Picture Effects button, where you can select additional preset styles and shadow, reflection, glow, soft edges, bevel, and 3-D rotation styles.

3. **Make sure that the photos are still selected, click the Picture Effects button in the Picture Styles group, point to Preset, then click Preset 4 (fourth column, first row)**

    The photos have a bevel and lighting style applied to them.

4. **Make sure that the photos are still selected, click the Recolor button in the Adjust group, point to each style under Color Modes, Dark Variations, and Light Variations to preview them, then click away from the gallery**

    The Recolor gallery includes a variety of color choices you can apply to any picture; Live Preview lets you sample them without making a selection. Note that the hues change depending on the theme applied to the presentation.

5. **Move to Slide 3, click the Insert tab, click the Picture button in the Illustrations group, navigate to where you store your Data Files, click giraffe.jpg, then click Insert**

    A photo of a giraffe is inserted in the slide.

6. **Drag the photo above the divider bar so it is next to the title, then click the Picture Tools Format tab**

7. **Click the Recolor button in the Adjust group, click Set Transparent Color, then click ⬚ in a blue part of the photo**

    When you click the image, it deletes all pixels matching that color, making those areas transparent, as shown in Figure E-15.

8. **Click the Brightness button in the Adjust group, click +10%, then save your work**

FIGURE E-14: Picture Style applied to photos

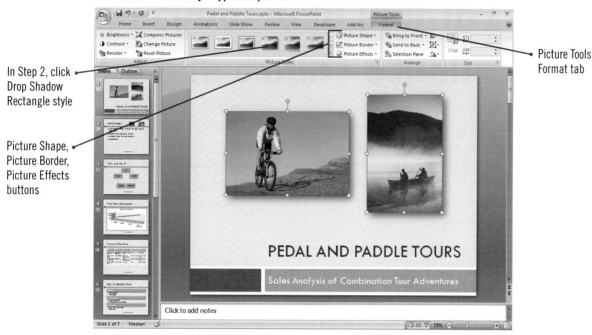

In Step 2, click Drop Shadow Rectangle style

Picture Shape, Picture Border, Picture Effects buttons

Picture Tools Format tab

FIGURE E-15: Color deleted from a picture

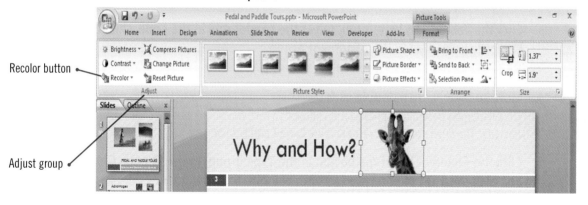

Recolor button

Adjust group

Embedding sound and video files

You can insert movie and sound files in a presentation from your hard drive, a Flash drive, a CD or DVD, or another storage device. Once a file is inserted, you choose whether to embed the file in the presentation or to link the file to the presentation. Embedding a file inserts the file in the presentation and thus significantly increases file size and can affect performance when someone plays the presentation. Linking a file avoids these issues, but you must provide a copy of that file whenever you transmit the presentation to another computer, whether via e-mail or on a CD. Generally, you should link a file if it is over 100 KB. This is easily accomplished using the Package for CD publishing feature; click the Office button, point to Publish, then click Package for CD. When you embed a file, you cannot modify it unless you open it in an appropriate application and then reinsert it in the slide show. When you link a file, any changes you make to the source file update the link automatically, which is useful if you use the same media in other PowerPoint presentations or other Office documents. By default, movies are always linked; you cannot embed them. However, you can embed an Adobe Flash animation in a slide. To add an Adobe Flash animation to a slide, you must first install the Flash Player on your computer and use the Developer tab on the Ribbon to add the appropriate ActiveX control.

Learning New Ways to Enhance Tables and Charts

In PowerPoint 2003, creating tables and charts was often time-consuming and you could not easily update data. Using tables created in other applications such as Word or Excel was also a challenge, because you could only paste a table in PowerPoint as an image. In 2007, you can easily paste a table created in another Office application, and the table automatically configures to the slide width and assumes the theme colors. Charts open automatically in an Excel spreadsheet, and you can choose whether to embed or link them. You can also apply a wide array of styles and other formatting options. ▨▨▨▨ In this lesson, modify the styles in a table and in a chart.

STEPS

1. **Click Slide 5, click the table, then click the Table Tools Design tab on the Ribbon, then point to a few styles in the Table Styles group to preview them**
   When you select a table, two contextual Table Tools tabs appear on the Ribbon, Design and Layout. The Table Tools Design tab includes Table Style Options such as hiding or displaying the Header row, Table Styles, and WordArt styles where you can format the table. See Figure E-16. The Layout tab includes options for working with the structure of a table, such as inserting rows and columns, adjusting cell margins, and so on.

   > **QUICK TIP**
   > A table is a grid-like arrangement of numeric values or data, a chart is a visual representation of data, and a SmartArt graphic is a visual representation of information and ideas.

2. **Click a table border so that no cell is selected, click the Effects button ▨▾ in the Table Styles group, point to Cell Bevel, then click Cool Slant (fourth column, first row)**
   An effect is applied to the table, giving the table cells a 3-D look.

3. **Click the Table Tools Layout tab, select the header row in the table, then click the Center Vertically button ▤ in the Alignment group**
   The header row text is centered vertically in the cells.

   > **QUICK TIP**
   > You can insert a chart by clicking the Insert Chart button in the Illustrations group of the Insert tab, or by clicking the icon in the content placeholder.

4. **Move to Slide 4, then double-click the chart**
   The Chart Tools Design tab appears on the Ribbon, where you can format the chart, change chart types, and edit data. The other contextual chart tabs are Layout and Format.

5. **Click the Change Chart Type button in the Type group, in the Change Chart Type dialog box click the 3-D Column type (seventh column, first row under Column), as shown in Figure E-17, then click OK**
   The new chart type is applied to the chart, giving it a 3-D appearance.

   > **QUICK TIP**
   > If Excel does not open tiled with PowerPoint, press [Alt][Tab] to switch programs.

6. **Click the Edit Data button in the Data group**
   After a few moments, Excel opens with the data in a spreadsheet and the two program windows appear side by side on the screen, as shown in Figure E-18. You can add or replace the data in Excel and then return to PowerPoint.

7. **Click cell B6, type 2000, then press [Enter]**
   The chart data in the slide updates automatically.

   > **QUICK TIP**
   > It is not necessary to save the spreadsheet in Excel; if you later edit the chart data from PowerPoint, the data opens in a new spreadsheet.

8. **Click the Office button ▨, then click Exit Excel**
   Excel closes, the PowerPoint window maximizes, and the chart in the slide updates.

9. **Save your work**

FIGURE E-16: Table Tools Design tab

Table Tools
Design tab

Table Styles
group

Table Shading,
Border, and
Effects buttons

Table Tools
Layout tab

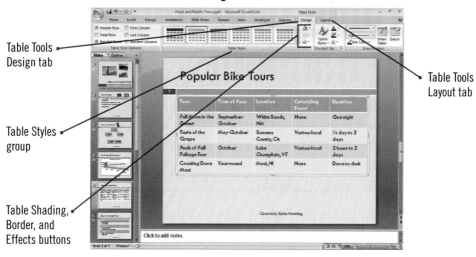

FIGURE E-17: Change Chart Type dialog box

Chart Tools
Design tab

Change Chart
Type dialog
box

Chart Tools
Format tab

Chart Tools
Layout tab

3-D Column type

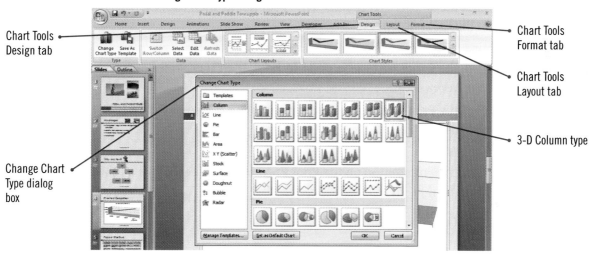

FIGURE E-18: Viewing a chart in PowerPoint and Excel

Click to open
spreadsheet
in Excel

Spreadsheet
open in Excel

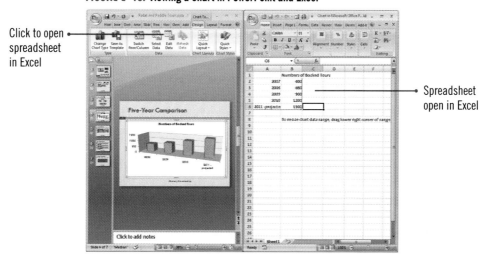

Learning New Ways to View Handouts

Printing a slide show, Speaker Notes, or Handouts has not changed significantly in PowerPoint 2007. However, you can now preview the elements you want to print without having to first open the Print dialog box. You can use features on the View tab to preview a layout or change previews.  In this lesson, select a handout layout, add a header, and then print out a handout of the slide show.

STEPS

1. **Click the View tab on the Ribbon, then click the Handout Master button in the Presentation Views group**

   The view changes to Handout Master view, where you can determine how the handouts will appear on a page and what information to include in the header or footer. The default layout for handouts appears in the window and the Handout Master tab is active on the Ribbon, as shown in Figure E-19, with commands for customizing your handouts. You can quickly change the page orientation, the number of slides per page, headers and footers, themes, and styles using this tab.

2. **Click the Header Placeholder, type your name, then click the Close Master View button in the Close group**

   The Handout Master layout closes.

3. **Click the Office button 🔘, point to Print, then click Print Preview**

   Print Preview opens.

4. **Click the Print What list arrow, compare your screen to Figure E-20, then click Handouts (4 Slides Per Page)**

   Print Preview shows four slides per page, as shown in Figure E-21.

5. **Click the Print button on the Print Preview tab, click OK in the Print dialog box, then close Print Preview**

6. **Save your work, then exit PowerPoint**

Understanding copyright

When adding images and other media to your presentations, be aware that copyright law may affect the legality of your use. Copyright applies to intellectual property, known as works of authorship, including books, Web pages, computer games, music, artwork, and photographs. Intellectual property is any idea or creation of the human mind. Copyright law protects the expression of an idea, but not the underlying facts or concepts. In other words, the general subject matter is not protected, but how you convey it is, such as several people photographing the same scene.

Fair use is an exception to copyright and permits the public to use copyrighted material for certain purposes without obtaining prior consent from the owner. Determining whether fair use applies to a work depends on its purpose, whether the work is factual or creative, how much you want to copy, and the effect on the work's value. Unauthorized use of protected work (such as downloading a photo or song) is known as copyright infringement, and can lead to legal problems.

Microsoft acquires artwork and sound files from third-party sources, but states that their clip art can be used for personal use, which includes school assignments, cards, and other noncommercial uses. You may not use their clip art to advertise your business or create a company logo.

FIGURE E-19: Viewing the Handout Master

Handout Master tab

Header placeholder

Date prints by default

Page number prints by default

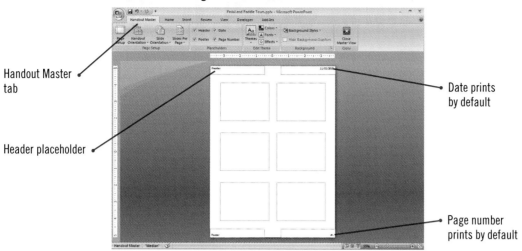

FIGURE E-20: Viewing Print Preview

In Step 4, click this option

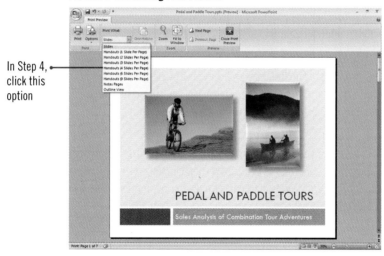

FIGURE E-21: Previewing four slides per page

Print button

Preview showing four slides

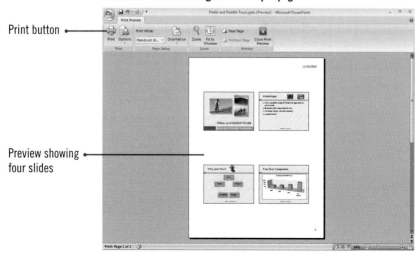

Learning Other New Features

PowerPoint 2007 has several new features that can help you create presentations efficiently and share them with a wide audience. Some features are no longer available, as described in Table E-3.  In this lesson, review additional new features of PowerPoint 2007.

DETAILS

As you use PowerPoint 2007, note these additional features and changes:

- **Custom layouts and placeholders**

  You can modify slide layouts by adding placeholders to them or creating a custom layout. Click the View tab, then click the Slide Master button in the Presentation Views group. You can click the Insert Layout button in the Edit Master group to add a custom layout to the Slide Master. You can click the Insert Placeholder button in the Master Layout group to add a placeholder to any slide layout. See Figure E-22.

- **Compatibility with previous versions**

  To save a PowerPoint 2007 presentation that is completely compatible with earlier versions of PowerPoint, click the Office button, point to Save As, then click PowerPoint 97-2003 Presentation. The Microsoft Office PowerPoint Compatibility Checker dialog box opens, listing the features that are not supported by earlier versions of PowerPoint. The features may no longer appear or not appear as well as they did in PowerPoint 2007. You can run the Compatibility Checker at any time by clicking the Office Button, clicking Prepare, and then clicking Run Compatibility Checker.

- **Inspecting a document**

  The Document Inspector includes several different Inspectors that you can use to find and remove different kinds of hidden data and personal information in your presentation, such as comments, objects that appear outside the slide area, presentation notes, and document properties (known as metadata).

- **Marking a presentation as final**

  After you've completed a presentation, you can use the Mark as Final command to make the presentation read-only and prevent changes by a future reader. Click the Office Button, point to Prepare, then click Mark as Final. When a presentation is marked as final, no one, not even you as the author, can make any changes to it and a Marked as Final icon appears in the status bar.

- **New viewing capabilities**

  You can enhance the presentation notes you've written in the Notes pane. On the View tab, click Notes Page view and then format text and add pictures or charts. Your enhancements are visible in Notes Page view and when you print and the notes, but they are not visible in Normal view.

- **Saving a presentation as a PDF or XPS file**

  To save a PowerPoint presentation as a PDF file, you must first install the 2007 Microsoft Office Add-in: Microsoft Save as PDF or XPS from the Download Center at www.microsoft.com. If you have earlier versions of Adobe Acrobat installed on your computer, you can create PDFs from Office applications without having to download the add-in. The Office add-in adds a PDF and XPS option to the Save As menu.

- **New Selection pane functionality**

  The Selection pane in PowerPoint 2007 lists all the objects on a slide in the order in which they are "stacked" in the slide. The top object in the list is the topmost or front-most, object on the slide. The Selection pane is very useful when you need to manage custom animations in a slide or when you group objects. You can move objects up or down and rename, hide, or show them. See Figure E-23. To open the Selection Pane, click the Home tab on the Ribbon, click the Select button in the Editing group, and then click Selection Pane. On the slide, you can now use common keyboard commands to group objects. To group objects, press [Ctrl][G]; to ungroup objects, press [Ctrl][Shift][G].

FIGURE E-22: Viewing the Insert Placeholder list on the Slide Master tab

Click to insert new layout

Click to insert new placeholder

FIGURE E-23: Slide objects in the Selection pane

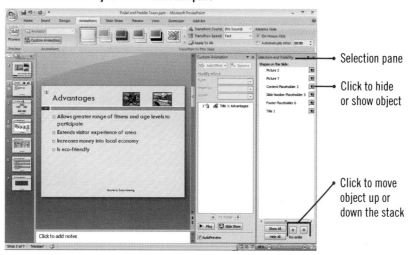

Selection pane

Click to hide or show object

Click to move object up or down the stack

TABLE E-3: Features in PowerPoint 2003 not available in PowerPoint 2007

feature in 2003	replacement
Allow fast saves	None
Auto-Content Wizard	Templates
From Scanner or Camera Option	Insert downloaded media
Macro recorder	Click the Macros button in the Code group of the Developer tab to open Visual Basic for Applications
Microsoft Producer	None
Office Assistant	Help window (the Assistant no longer exists)
Presentation Broadcasting	None
Send for Review	E-mail the presentation by clicking Office button, pointing to Send, then clicking E-mail
Speaker notes dialog box during slide show	None
Style Checker	None
Summary slide	None
Text Highlight Option	Shape Fill
Title Master	Layouts in Slide Master

Practice

If you have a SAM user profile, you may have access to hands-on instruction, practice, and assessment of the skills covered in this unit. Log in to your SAM account (http://sam2007.course.com/) to launch any assigned training activities or exams that relate to the skills covered in this unit.

▼ CONCEPTS REVIEW

Match the items below with the elements in Figure E-24.

FIGURE E-24

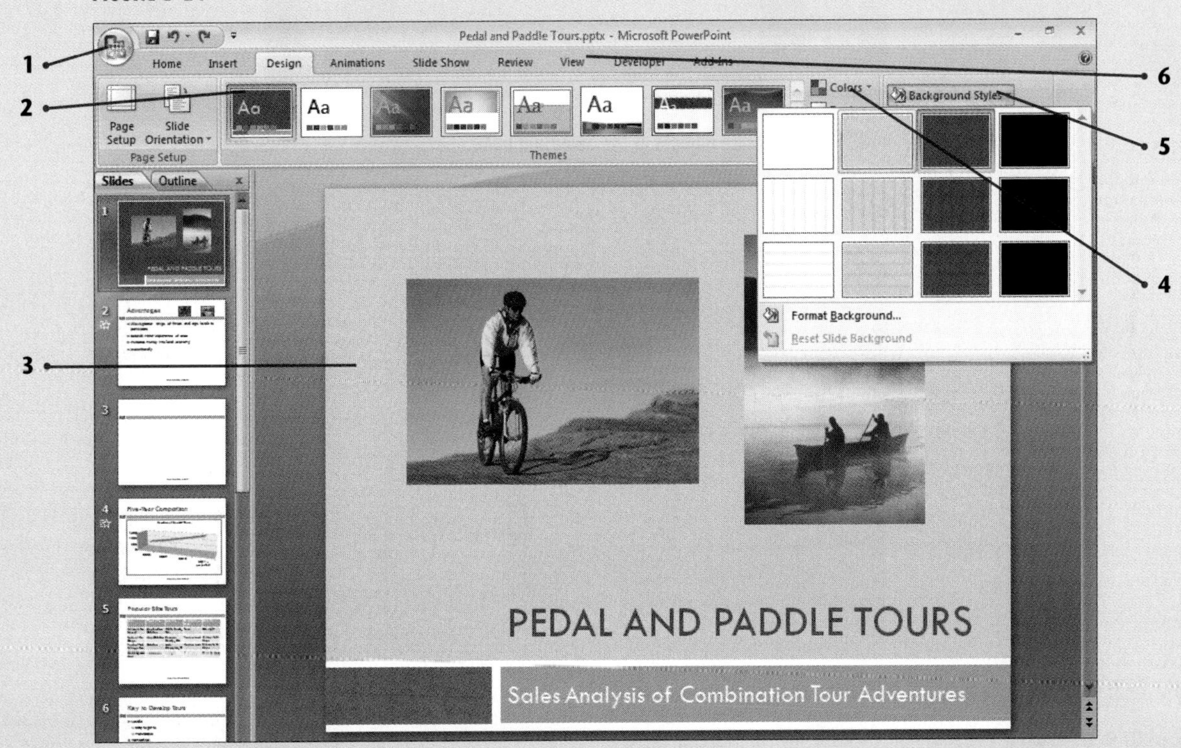

a. Click to open a menu where you can save a presentation as a PDF

b. Click to change the Theme Colors

c. Click to open a tab containing a command to edit the slide master

d. Points to the currently selected theme

e. Click to change the background color

f. Shows a live preview of a style

▼ SKILLS REVIEW

1. Learn new ways to perform program tasks.

a. Start PowerPoint, open the file E-2.pptx from the drive and folder where you store your Data Files, then save it as **Small Business Recycling**.

b. Add a new slide after Slide 4.

c. Duplicate Slide 6, then delete it.

d. Click the Animations tab on the Ribbon, open the Transitions gallery, preview several transitions, then apply a Push Up slide transition under Push and Cover to all slides in the presentation.

e. Save your work.

2. Learn to use new themes and styles.

a. Click the Design tab on the Ribbon, open the Themes gallery, preview several styles, then apply the Flow theme to the presentation.

b. Open the Background Styles gallery, then apply Style 7 to the presentation.

c. Open the Theme Fonts gallery, then apply the Solstice Theme Fonts to the presentation.

d. Save your work.

3. Learn new ways to enhance text and shapes.

FIGURE E-25

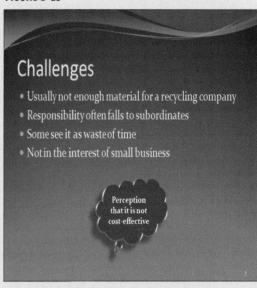

a. Move to Slide 3, copy the text **Perception that it is not cost-effective**, then delete the text box.

b. Click the Shapes button arrow in the Drawing group on the Home tab, scroll down the gallery, then click Cloud Callout in the Callouts section.

c. Click the slide beneath the bulleted list, then paste the text in the shape. (*Hint*: The text does not fit in the shape.)

d. Drag a sizing handle of the shape until the text fits in the shape.

e. Use a button in the Arrange group on the Drawing Tools Format tab to center-align the text box.

f. Change the font color to white and center the text.

g. Open the Shape Effects gallery, apply the Preset 5 effect to the text box, then click away from the text box.

h. Compare your screen to Figure E-25, then save your work.

4. Learn to create SmartArt graphics.

a. Move to Slide 5, then add the title **Waste Pyramid** to the slide.

b. Open the SmartArt dialog box, then create a Pyramid List SmartArt graphic.

c. Enter the following text in each bullet: **Minimize**, **Reuse**, **Recycle**, **Recover Energy**, **Landfill**. (*Hint*: Press [Enter] after the third bullet to add a new line.)

FIGURE E-26

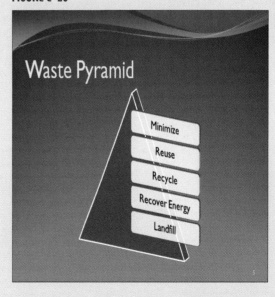

d. Open the SmartArt Styles gallery, apply the Brick Scene style to the graphic, click away from the graphic, then compare your screen to Figure E-26.

FIGURE E-27

e. Move to Slide 6, then convert the bulleted text to a Process Funnel SmartArt graphic in the Process category. (*Hint*: Click More SmartArt Graphics in the Convert to SmartArt Graphic gallery.)

f. Open the SmartArt Styles gallery, then apply the Powder style under 3-D to the graphic.

g. Click away from the graphic, compare your screen to Figure E-27, then save your work.

5. **Learn new ways to enhance pictures.**

a. Move to Slide 4, select the photo, open the Picture Styles gallery, then apply the Rounded Diagonal Corner, White style to the photo.

b. Open the Recolor gallery, then apply the Accent color 1 Light style under Light Variations to the photo.

c. Move to Slide 1, then select the photo.

d. Adjust the Contrast to +10%, then compress all the pictures in the presentation, using the default settings.

e. Open the Picture Effects gallery, then apply the Accent color 2, 18 pt glow style under Glow to the photo.

f. Save your work.

6. **Learn new ways to enhance tables and charts.**

a. Move to Slide 2, then select the table.

b. Open the Table Styles gallery, then apply the Themed Style 1–Accent 2 style (third column, first row under Best Match for Document) to the table.

c. Open the Effects gallery, open the Shadow palette, then apply the Below style (third column, first row under Perspective) to the table.

d. Move to Slide 7, select the chart, then change the chart type to Clustered Cylinder in the Column category.

e. Edit the data in Excel. Type **Plastics** in cell A7, type **80** in cell B7, then press [Enter].

f. Verify that the new data is added to the chart. If the new column does not appear automatically, drag the blue data border in Excel down one row, to include cells A7 and B7.

g. Exit Excel, then in PowerPoint, open the Chart Styles gallery, apply Style 20 to the chart, then click away from the chart.

h. Compare your screen to Figure E-28, save your work, then view the presentation in Slide Show view.

7. Learn new ways to view handouts.

a. View the presentation in Handout Master view.

b. On the Insert tab, use a command in the Text group to open the Header and Footer dialog box.

c. Click the Footer check box to add a checkmark, type your name in the Footer text box, then click Apply to All.

d. View the presentation in Print Preview. Click the Print What list arrow, then change the layout to three slides per page.

e. Print the presentation with three slides per page.

f. Close Print Preview, save your work, then exit PowerPoint.

FIGURE E-28

▼ VISUAL WORKSHOP

Start a new presentation using the Blank Presentation template, then create and format the slide shown in Figure E-29. Save the presentation as **Best Beach Vacations** to the drive and folder where you store your Data Files. Add your name to the footer, then print the slide. (*Hint*: You will need to change the slide layout, apply a theme, and change the background of the slide, in addition to creating the graphic.) Print the slide, then save and close the file.

FIGURE E-29

Upgrading Command Reference

Word 2003 to 2007 Command Reference

Use this table to locate a Word 2003 menu command where available. Not all commands have a direct equivalent in Word 2007.

Note: Only top-level Word 2003 menu commands are listed. If two Ribbon locations are listed, you'll find one or more Word 2003 commands in each location.

Word 2003 menu	Word 2003 command	Word 2007 Ribbon location
File menu	New	Office button
	Open	Office button
	Close	Office button
	Save	Office button
	Save As	Office button
	Save As Web page	Office button/Save As dialog box
	File Search	No direct equivalent
	Permission	Office button/Prepare menu
	Versions	No direct equivalent
	Web Page Preview	Office button/Word Options dialog box/Customize category (add button to Quick Access toolbar)
	Page Setup	Page Layout tab
	Print Preview	Office button
	Print	Office button
	Send To	Office button/Send menu
	Properties	Office button/Prepare menu
	Exit	Office button
Edit menu	Undo	Quick Access toolbar
	Redo	Quick Access toolbar
	Cut	Home tab
	Copy	Home tab
	Office Clipboard	Home tab
	Paste Special	Home tab
	Paste as Hyperlink	Home tab
	Clear Formats	Home tab
	Clear Contents	No direct equivalent
	Select All	Home tab
	Find	Home tab
	Replace	Home tab
	Go To	Home tab
	Links	Office button, Prepare menu
	Object	Contextual tabs
View menu	Normal	No direct equivalent
	Web Layout	View tab
	Print Layout	View tab
	Reading Layout	View tab
	Outline	View tab
	Task Pane	No direct equivalent
	Toolbars	No direct equivalent
	Ruler	View tab
	Document Map	View tab
	Thumbnails	View tab

Word 2003 menu	Word 2003 command	Word 2007 Ribbon location
	Header and Footer	Insert tab
	Footnotes	References tab
	Markup	Review tab
	HTML Source	No direct equivalent
	Full Screen	View tab
	Zoom	View tab, Zoom slider
Insert menu	Break	Insert tab
	Page Numbers	Insert tab
	Date and Time	Insert tab
	AutoText	Insert tab/QuickParts button
	Field	Insert tab/QuickParts button
	Symbol	Insert tab
	Comment	Review tab
	Number	Insert tab
	Reference	References tab
	Web Component	Office button/Word Options dialog box/Customize category (add button to Quick Access toolbar)
	Picture	Insert tab, Review tab
	Diagram	Insert tab/SmartArt button
	Text Box	Insert tab
	File	Insert tab/Object button
	Object	Insert tab
	Bookmark	Insert tab
	Hyperlink	Insert tab
Format menu	Font	Home tab
	Paragraph	Home tab
	Bullets and Numbering	Home tab
	Borders and Shading	Home tab
	Columns	Page Layout tab
	Tabs	Page Layout tab
	Drop Cap	Insert tab
	Text Direction	Table Tools Layout tab (for table text); Text Box Tools Format tab (for a text box)
	Change Case	Home tab
	Background	Page Layout tab
	Theme	Page Layout tab
	Frames	Office button/Word Options dialog box/Customize category (add button to Quick Access toolbar)
	AutoFormat	Office button/Word Options dialog box/Customize and Proofing tabs
	Styles and Formatting	Home tab
	Reveal Formatting	Office button/Word Options dialog box/Customize category (add button to Quick Access toolbar)
	Object	Contextual tab for selected object
Tools menu	Spelling and Grammar	Review tab
	Research	Review tab
	Language	Review tab
	Word Count	Review tab
	AutoSummarize	Office button/Word Options dialog box/Customize category (add button to the Quick Access toolbar)
	Speech	No direct equivalent
	Shared Workspace	No direct equivalent
	Track Changes	Review tab
	Compare and Merge Documents	Review tab
	Protect Document	Developer tab, Review tab

Word 2003 menu	Word 2003 command	Word 2007 Ribbon location
	Online Collaboration	No direct equivalent
	Letters and Mailings	Mailings tab
	Macro	Developer tab
	Templates and Add-Ins	Developer tab
	AutoCorrect Options	Office button/Word Options dialog box/Proofing category
	Customize	Office button/Word Options dialog box/Customize category
	Options	Office button/Word Options dialog box
Table menu	Draw Table	Insert tab
	Insert	Insert tab, Table Tools Layout tab
	Delete	Table Tools Layout tab
	Select	Table Tools Layout tab
	Merge Cells	Table Tools Layout tab
	Split Cells	Table Tools Layout tab
	Split Table	Table Tools Layout tab
	Table AutoFormat	Table Tools Design tab/Table Styles group
	AutoFit	Table Tools Layout tab
	Heading Rows Repeat	Table Tools Layout tab
	Convert	Insert tab, Table Tools Layout tab
	Sort	Table Tools Layout tab
	Formula	Table Tools Layout tab
	Show Gridlines	Table Tools Layout tab
	Table Properties	Table Tools Layout tab
Window menu	New Window	View tab
	Arrange All	View tab
	Compare Side by Side with	View tab
	Split	View tab
	Currently Open Documents	View tab
Help menu	Microsoft Office Word Help	Question mark button at right side of Ribbon
	Show the Office Assistant	No direct equivalent
	Microsoft Office Online	Office button/Word Options dialog box/Resources category
	Contact Us	Office button/Word Options dialog box/Resources category
	Check for Updates	Office button/Word Options dialog box/Resources category
	Detect and Repair	Office button/Word Options dialog box/Resources category

Excel 2003 to 2007 Command Reference

Use this table to locate an Excel 2003 menu command where available. Not all commands have a direct equivalent in Excel 2007.

Note: Only top-level Excel 2003 menu commands are listed. If two Ribbon locations are listed, you'll find one or more Excel 2003 commands in each location.

Excel 2003 menu	Excel 2003 Command	Excel 2007 Ribbon location
File menu	New	Office button
	Open	Office button
	Close	Office button
	Save	Office button
	Save As	Office button
	Save As Web Page	Office button/Save As dialog box
	Save As Workspace	View tab
	File Search	No direct equivalent
	Permission	Office button/Prepare menu
	Web Page Preview	Office button/Excel Options dialog box/Customize Quick Access toolbar

Excel 2003 menu	Excel 2003 Command	Excel 2007 Ribbon location
	Page Setup	Page Layout tab
	Print Area	Page Layout tab
	Print Preview	Office button
	Print	Office button
	Send To	Office button/Send menu
	Properties	Office button
	Exit	Office button
Edit menu	Undo	Quick Access toolbar
	Redo	Quick Access toolbar
	Cut	Home tab
	Copy	Home tab
	Office Clipboard	Home tab
	Paste	Home tab
	Paste Special	Home tab
	Paste as Hyperlink	Home tab
	Fill	Home tab
	Clear	Home tab
	Delete	Home tab
	Delete Sheet	Home tab
	Move or Copy Sheet	Home tab
	Find	Home tab
	Replace	Home tab
	Go To	Home tab
	Links	Office button
	Object	Contextual tabs
View menu	Normal	View tab
	Page Break Preview	View tab
	Task Pane	No direct equivalent
	Toolbars	No direct equivalent
	Formula Bar	View tab
	Status Bar	Displayed by default
	Header and Footer	Insert tab
	Comments	Review tab
	Custom Views	View tab
	Full Screen	View tab
	Zoom	View tab
Insert menu	Cells	Home tab
	Rows	Home tab
	Columns	Home tab
	Worksheet	Home tab
	Chart	Insert tab
	Symbol	Insert tab
	Page Break	Page Layout tab
	Function	Formulas tab
	Name	Formulas tab
	Ink Annotations	Review tab (Tablet PC only)
	Comment	Review tab
	Picture	Insert tab; From Scanner or Camera has no direct equivalent
	Diagram	Insert tab/SmartArt button
	Object	Insert tab
	Hyperlink	Insert tab

Excel 2003 menu	Excel 2003 Command	Excel 2007 Ribbon location
Format menu	Cell	Home tab
	Row	Home tab
	Column	Home tab
	Sheet	Home tab
	AutoFormat	Home tab
	Conditional Formatting	Home tab
	Style	Home tab
Tools menu	Spelling	Review tab
	Research	Review tab
	Error Checking	Formulas tab
	Speech	No direct equivalent
	Shared Workspace	No direct equivalent
	Share Workbook	Review tab
	Track Changes	Review tab
	Compare and Merge Workbooks Protection	Office button/Excel Options/Customize Quick Access toolbar; Review tab
	Online Collaboration	No direct equivalent
	Goal Seek	Data tab
	Scenarios	Data tab
	Formula Auditing	Formulas tab
	Macro	Developer tab
	Add-Ins	Add-Ins tab
	AutoCorrect Options	Office button
	Customize	Office button/Excel Options
	Options	Office button/Excel Options
Data menu	Sort	Data tab
	Filter	Data tab
	Form	Office button/Excel Options
	Subtotals	Data tab
	Validation	Data tab
	Table	Data tab, What-If Analysis button in Data Tools group
	Text to Columns	Data tab
	Consolidate	Data tab
	Group and Outline	Data tab
	PivotTable and PivotChart Report	Insert tab
	Import External Data	Data tab; Office button/Excel Options/Customize Quick Access toolbar
	List	Insert tab/Table command
	XML	Data tab/From Other Sources button; Developer tab/XML group; Office button/Save As
	Refresh Data	Data tab
Chart menu	Chart Type	Chart Tools Design tab
	Source Data	Chart Tools Design tab
	Chart Options	Chart Tools Layout tab
	Location	Chart Tools Design tab
	Add Data	Chart Tools Design tab
	Add Trendline	Chart Tools Layout tab
	3-D View	Chart Tools Layout tab
Window menu	New Window	View tab
	Arrange	View tab
	Compare Side by Side with	View tab
	Hide	View tab
	Unhide	View tab
	Split	View tab

Excel 2003 menu	Excel 2003 Command	Excel 2007 Ribbon location
	Freeze Panes/Unfreeze Panes	View tab
	List of Windows	View tab
Help menu	Microsoft Office Excel Help	Question mark button at right side of Ribbon
	Show the Office Assistant	No direct equivalent
	Microsoft Office Online	Office button/Excel Options/Resources group
	Contact Us	Office button/Excel Options/Resources group
	Check for Updates	Office button/Excel Options/Resources group
	Detect and Repair	Office button/Excel Options/Resources group
	Activate Product	Office button/Excel Options/Resources group
	Customer Feedback Options	Office button/Excel Options/Trust Center
	About Microsoft Excel	Office button/Excel Options/Resources group

Access 2003 to 2007 Command Reference

Use this table to locate an Access 2003 menu command where available. Not all commands have a direct equivalent in Access 2007.

Note: Only top-level Access 2003 menu commands are listed. If two Ribbon locations are listed, you'll find one or more Access 2003 commands in each location.

Access 2003 menu	Access 2003 Command	Access 2007 Ribbon location
File menu	New	Office button
	Open	Office button
	Get External Data	External Data tab
	Close	Office button
	Save	Quick Access toolbar; Office button
	Save As	Office button
	Backup Database	Office button, Manage
	Export	External Data tab
	File Search	No direct equivalent
	Page Setup	Office button/Print Preview; Page Layout tab
	Print Preview	Office button
	Print	Office button
	Send To	Office button
	Database Properties	Office button, Manage
	Exit	Office button
Edit menu	Undo	Quick Access toolbar
	Redo	Quick Access toolbar
	Cut	Home tab
	Copy	Home tab
	Office Clipboard	Home tab
	Paste	Home tab
	Paste Special	Home tab
	Paste as Hyperlink	No equivalent
	Delete	Home tab
	Delete (*object*)	Home tab
	Select Record	Home tab
	Select All	Home tab
	Find	Home tab
	Replace	Home tab
	Go To	Home tab
	OLE/DDE Links	No equivalent

Access 2003 menu	Access 2003 Command	Access 2007 Ribbon location
View menu	Design View	Home tab
	Form View/SQL View/Print Preview	Home tab
	Datasheet View	Home tab
	PivotTable View	Home tab
	PivotChart View	Home tab
	Subreport in New Window	Report Design Tools Design tab
	Layout Preview	Home tab
	Properties	Design tab, Arrange tab
	Object Dependencies	Database Tools tab, Datasheet tab
	Field List	Design tab
	Sorting and Grouping	Design tab
	Code	Database Tools tab
	Indexes	Design tab
	Ruler	Report Design Tools Arrange tab
	Grid	Report Design Tools Arrange tab
	Toolbox	Report Design Tools Design tab
	Page Header/Footer	Report Design Tools Arrange tab
	Report Header/Footer	Report Design Tools Arrange tab
	Task Pane	Home tab
	Toolbars	No equivalent
	Zoom	Print Preview
	Pages	Print Preview
Insert menu	Table; Query; Form; Report; Page; Macro	Create tab
	New Record	Datasheet tab, Design tab
	Column/Row	Datasheet tab, Design tab
	Page Numbers	Design tab
	Date and Time	Design tab, Formatting tab
	Lookup Column/Lookup Field	Datasheet tab
	Hyperlink	Report Design Tools Design tab; Form Design Tools Design tab
	Subdatasheet	Insert tab
	Module; Class Module	Create tab; Macro
	Chart	Design tab
	Picture	Design tab, Format tab
	AutoForm; AutoReport	Create tab
	Object	Design tab
	ActiveX Control	Design tab
	Hyperlink	Design tab
Format menu	Font	Home tab
	Row Height	Home tab
	Column Width	Home tab
	AutoFormat	Arrange tab, Format tab
	Set Control Defaults	No equivalent
	Change To	No equivalent
	Conditional Formatting	Design tab
	Rename Column	Datasheet tab
	Hide Columns	Home tab
	Unhide Columns	Home tab
	Freeze Columns	Home tab
	Unfreeze Columns	Home tab
	Subdatasheet	Home tab
	Snap to Grid	Arrange tab
	Align	Arrange tab
	Size	Arrange tab
	Horizontal Spacing	Arrange tab
	Vertical Spacing	Arrange tab
	Group	Arrange tab

Access 2003 menu	Access 2003 Command	Access 2007 Ribbon location
	Ungroup	Arrange tab
	Bring to Front	Arrange tab
	Send to Back	Arrange tab
Query menu	Run	Design tab
	Show Table	Design tab
	Remove Table	No equivalent
	Select Query	Design tab
	Crosstab Query	Design tab
	Make-Table Query	Design tab
	Update Query	Design tab
	Append Query	Design tab
	Delete Query	Design tab
	SQL Specific	Design tab
	Parameters	Design tab
Records menu	Filter	Home tab
	Sort	Home tab
	Apply Filter/Sort; Remove Filter/Sort	Home tab
	Save Record	Home tab
	Refresh	Home tab
	Data Entry	No equivalent
Tools menu	Spelling	Home tab
	Office Links	External Data tab
	Online Collaboration	No direct equivalent
	Relationships	Database Tools tab
	Analyze	Database Tools tab
	Database Utilities	Database Tools tab; Office button/Access Options
	Security	Database Tools tab; Office button/Access Options
	Replication	No direct equivalent
	Startup	Office button/Access Options
	Macro	Database Tools tab
	ActiveX Controls	Office button/Access Options
	Add-Ins	Office button/Access Options
	AutoCorrect Options	Office button/Access Options
	Customize	Office button/Access Options
	Options	Office button/Access Options
Window menu	Tile Horizontally	Home tab
	Tile Vertically	Home tab
	Cascade	Home tab
	Arrange Icons	Home tab
	Hide	No direct equivalent
	Unhide	No direct equivalent
Help menu	Microsoft Office Access Help	Question mark button at right side of Ribbon
	Show the Office Assistant	No direct equivalent
	Microsoft Office Online	Office button/Access Options/Resources group
	Access Developer Resources	Office button/New; Office button/Access Options/Resources group
	Contact Us	Office button/Access Options/Resources group
	Sample Databases	Office button/New
	Check for Updates	Office button/Access Options/Resources group
	Detect and Repair	Office button/Manage
	Activate Product	Office button/Access Options/Resources group
	Customer Feedback Options	Office button/Access Options/Trust Center group
	About Microsoft Office Access	Office button/Access Options/Resources group

PowerPoint 2003 to 2007 Command Reference

Use this table to locate a PowerPoint 2003 menu command where available. Not all commands have a direct equivalent in PowerPoint 2007.

Note: Only top-level PowerPoint 2003 menu commands are listed. If two Ribbon locations are listed, you'll find one or more PowerPoint 2003 commands in each location.

PowerPoint 2003 menu	PowerPoint 2003 command	PowerPoint 2007 location
File menu	New	Office button
	Open	Office button
	Close	Office button
	Save	Quick Access toolbar
	Save As	Office button
	Save As Web Page	Office button/Save As dialog box
	File Search	Use the Operating System's search function
	Permission	Office button/Prepare menu
	Web Page Preview	Office button/PowerPoint Options
	Package for CD	Office button/Publish menu
	Web Page Preview	Office button/PowerPoint Options
	Page Setup	Design tab
	Print Preview	Office button
	Print	Office button
	Send To	Office button
	Properties	Office button/Prepare menu
	Exit	Office button
Edit menu	Undo	Quick Access toolbar
	Redo	Quick Access toolbar
	Cut	Home tab
	Copy	Home tab
	Office Clipboard	Home tab
	Paste	Home tab
	Paste Special	Home tab
	Paste as Hyperlink	Home tab
	Clear	Office button/PowerPoint Options
	Select All	Home tab
	Delete Slide	Home tab
	Duplicate	Home tab
	Find	Home tab
	Replace	Home tab
	Go To Property	PowerPoint Options/Customize
	Links	Office button
	Object	Double-click object, look for contextual tabs
View menu	Normal	View tab (or status bar)
	Slide Sorter	View tab (or status bar)
	Slide Show	View tab (or status bar)
	Notes Page	View tab
	Master	View tab
	Color/Grayscale	View tab
	Task Pane	No direct equivalent
	Toolbars	Contextual tabs
	Ruler	View tab
	Grids and Guides	View tab
	Header and Footer	Insert tab
	Markup	Review tab
	Zoom	View tab (or Zoom slider)

PowerPoint 2003 menu	PowerPoint 2003 command	PowerPoint 2007 location
Insert menu	New Slide	Home tab
	Duplicate Slide	Home tab/New Slide button arrow
	Slide Number	Insert tab
	Ink Annotations	Review tab
	Date and Time	Insert Tab
	Symbol	Insert tab
	Comment	Review tab
	Slide From Files	Home tab/New Slide button arrow/Reuse Slides
	Slide From Outline	Home tab/New Slide button arrow/Slides from Outline
	Picture	Insert tab
	Diagram	Insert tab/SmartArt button
	Text Box	Insert tab
	Movies and Sounds	Insert tab
	Chart	Insert tab
	Table	Insert tab
	Object	Insert tab
	Hyperlink	Insert tab
Format menu	Font	Home tab
	Bullets and Numbering	Home tab
	Alignment	Home tab
	Line Spacing	Home tab
	Change Case	Home tab
	Replace Fonts	Home tab
	Slide Design	Design tab
	Slide Layout	Home tab
	Background	Design tab
	Object	Contextual tabs
Tools menu	Spelling	Review tab
	Research	Review tab
	Thesaurus	Review tab
	Language	Review tab
	Shared Workspace	No direct equivalent
	Compare and Merge Presentations	No direct equivalent
	Online Collaboration	No direct equivalent
	Macro	View tab or Developer tab
	Add-Ins	Add-Ins tab
	AutoCorrect Options	Office button/PowerPoint Options
	Customize	Office button/PowerPoint Options
	Options	Office button/PowerPoint Options/Prepare menu
Slide Show menu	View Show	Slide Show tab
	Set Up Show	Slide Show tab
	Rehearse Timings	Slide Show tab
	Action Buttons	Home tab
	Action Settings	Insert Tab
	Animation Schemes	Animation tab
	Custom Animation	Animation tab
	Slide Transitions	Animation tab
	Hide Slide	Slide Show tab
	Custom Shows	Slide Show tab
Window menu	New Window	View tab
	Arrange All	View tab
	Cascade	View tab
	Next Pane	No direct equivalent
	List of Windows	View tab

PowerPoint 2003 menu	PowerPoint 2003 command	PowerPoint 2007 location
Help menu	Microsoft Office PowerPoint Help	Question mark button at right side of Ribbon
	Show the Office Assistant	No direct equivalent
	Microsoft Office Online	Office button/PowerPoint Options
	Contact Us	Office button/PowerPoint Options
	Check for Updates	Office button/PowerPoint Options
	Detect and Repair	Office button/PowerPoint Options
	Activate Product	Office button/PowerPoint Options
	Customer Feedback Options	Office button/PowerPoint Options
	About Microsoft PowerPoint	Office button/PowerPoint Options/Trust Center

Restoring Defaults in Windows Vista and Disabling and Enabling Windows Aero

Windows Vista is the most recent version of the Windows operating system. An operating system controls the way you work with your computer, supervises running programs, and provides tools for completing your computing tasks. After surveying millions of computer users, Microsoft incorporated their suggestions to make Windows Vista secure, reliable, and easy to use. In fact, Windows Vista is considered the most secure version of Windows yet. Other improvements include a powerful new search feature that lets you quickly search for files and programs from the Start menu and most windows, tools that simplify accessing the Internet, especially with a wireless connection, and multimedia programs that let you enjoy, share, and organize music, photos, and recorded TV. Finally, Windows Vista offers lots of visual appeal with its transparent, three-dimensional design in the Aero experience. ▓▓▓ This appendix explains how to make sure you are using the Windows Vista default settings for appearance, personalization, security, hardware, and sound and to enable and disable Windows Aero. For more information on Windows Aero, go to *www.microsoft.com/windowsvista/experiences/aero.mspx*.

OBJECTIVES

- Restore the defaults in the Appearance and Personalization section
- Restore the defaults in the Security section
- Restore the defaults in the Hardware and Sound section
- Disable Windows Aero
- Enable Windows Aero

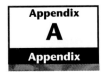

Restoring the Defaults in the Appearance and Personalization Section

The following instructions require a default Windows Vista Ultimate installation and the student logged in with an Administrator account. All of the following settings can be changed by accessing the Control Panel.

STEPS

- To restore the defaults in the Personalization section

  1. Click Start, and then click Control Panel. Click Appearance and Personalization, click Personalization, and then compare your screen to Figure A-1

  2. In the Personalization window, click Windows Color and Appearance, select the Default color, and then click OK

  3. In the Personalization window, click Mouse Pointers. In the Mouse Properties dialog box, on the Pointers tab, select Windows Aero (system scheme) in the Scheme drop-down list, and then click OK

  4. In the Personalization window, click Theme. Select Windows Vista from the Theme drop-down list, and then click OK

  5. In the Personalization window, click Display Settings. In the Display Settings dialog box, drag the Resolution bar to 1024 by 768 pixels, and then click OK

FIGURE A-1

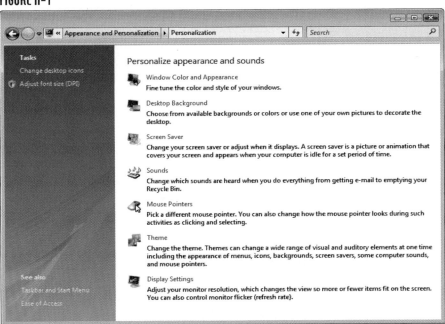

- To restore the defaults in the Taskbar and Start Menu section

    1. Click Start, and then click Control Panel. Click Appearance and Personalization, click Taskbar and Start Menu, and then compare your screen to Figure A-2

    2. In the Taskbar and Start Menu Properties dialog box, on the Taskbar tab, click to select all checkboxes except for "Auto-hide the taskbar"

    3. On the Start Menu tab, click to select the Start menu radio button and check all items in the Privacy section

    4. In the System icons section on the Notification Area tab, click to select all of the checkboxes except for "Power"

    5. On the Toolbars tab, click to select Quick Launch, none of the other items should be checked

    6. Click OK to close the Taskbar and Start Menu Properties dialog box

- To restore the defaults in the Folder Options section

    1. Click Start, and then click Control Panel. Click Appearance and Personalization, click Folder Options, and then compare your screen to Figure A-3

    2. In the Folder Options dialog box, on the General tab, click to select Show preview and filters in the Tasks section, click to select Open each folder in the same window in the Browse folders section, and click to select Double-click to open an item (single-click to select) in the Click items as follows section

    3. On the View tab, click the Reset Folders button, and then click Yes in the Folder views dialog box. Then click the Restore Defaults button

    4. On the Search tab, click the Restore Defaults button

    5. Click OK to close the Folder Options dialog box

- To restore the defaults in the Windows Sidebar Properties section

    1. Click Start, and then click Control Panel. Click Appearance and Personalization, click Windows Sidebar Properties, and then compare your screen to Figure A-4

    2. In the Windows Sidebar Properties dialog box, on the Sidebar tab, click to select Start Sidebar when Windows starts. In the Arrangement section, click to select Right, and then click to select 1 in the Display Sidebar on monitor drop-down list

    3. Click OK to close the Windows Sidebar Properties dialog box

FIGURE A-2

FIGURE A-3

FIGURE A-4

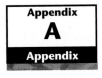

Restoring the Defaults in the Security Section

The following instructions require a default Windows Vista Ultimate installation and the student logged in with an Administrator account. All of the following settings can be changed by accessing the Control Panel.

STEPS

- To restore the defaults in the Windows Firewall section

  1. Click Start, and then click Control Panel. Click Security, click Windows Firewall, and then compare your screen to Figure A-5

  2. In the Windows Firewall dialog box, click Change settings. If the User Account Control dialog box appears, click Continue

  3. In the Windows Firewall Settings dialog box, click the Advanced tab. Click Restore Defaults, then click Yes in the Restore Defaults Confirmation dialog box

  4. Click OK to close the Windows Firewall Settings dialog box, and then close the Windows Firewall window

- To restore the defaults in the Internet Options section

  1. Click Start, and then click Control Panel. Click Security, click Internet Options, and then compare your screen to Figure A-6

  2. In the Internet Properties dialog box, on the General tab, click the Use default button. Click the Settings button in the Tabs section, and then click the Restore defaults button in the Tabbed Browsing Settings dialog box. Click OK to close the Tabbed Browsing Settings dialog box

  3. On the Security tab of the Internet Properties dialog box, click to uncheck the Enable Protected Mode checkbox, if necessary. Click the Default level button in the Security level for this zone section. If possible, click the Reset all zones to default level button

  4. On the Programs tab, click the Make default button in the Default web browser button for Internet Explorer, if possible. If Office is installed, Microsoft Office Word should be selected in the HTML editor drop-down list

  5. On the Advanced tab, click the Restore advanced settings button in the Settings section. Click the Reset button in the Reset Internet Explorer settings section, and then click Reset in the Reset Internet Explorer Settings dialog box

  6. Click Close to close the Reset Internet Explorer Settings dialog box, and then click OK to close the Internet Properties dialog box

FIGURE A-5

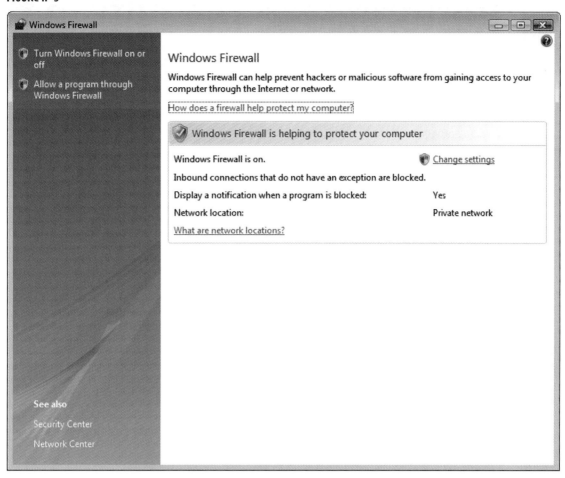

FIGURE A-6

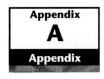

Restoring the Defaults in the Hardware and Sound Section

The following instructions require a default Windows Vista Ultimate installation and the student logged in with an Administrator account. All of the following settings can be changed by accessing the Control Panel.

STEPS

- To restore the defaults in the Autoplay section
    1. Click Start, and then click Control Panel. Click Hardware and Sound, click Autoplay, and then compare your screen to Figure A-7. Scroll down and click the Reset all defaults button in the Devices section at the bottom of the window, and then click Save

- To restore the defaults in the Sound section
    1. Click Start, and then click Control Panel. Click Hardware and Sound, click Sound, and then compare your screen to Figure A-8
    2. In the Sound dialog box, on the Sounds tab, select Windows Default from the Sound Scheme drop-down list, and then click OK

- To restore the defaults in the Mouse section
    1. Click Start, and then click Control Panel. Click Hardware and Sound, click Mouse, and then compare your screen to Figure A-9
    2. In the Mouse Properties dialog box, on the Pointers tab, select Windows Aero (system scheme) from the Scheme drop-down list
    3. Click OK to close the Mouse Properties dialog box

FIGURE A-7

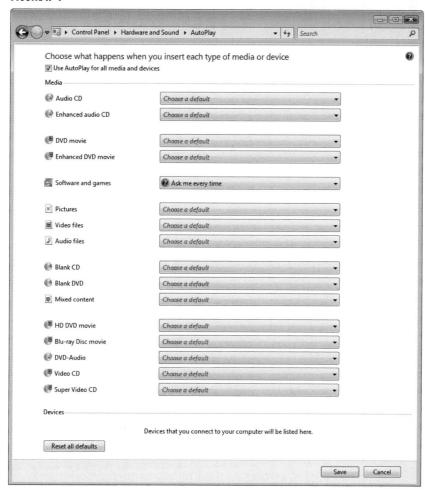

FIGURE A-8

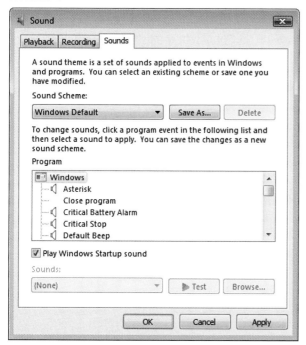

FIGURE A-9

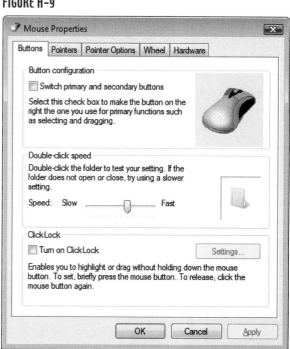

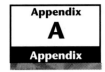

Disabling and Enabling Windows Aero

Unlike prior versions of Windows, Windows Vista provides two distinct user interface experiences: a "basic" experience for entry-level systems and more visually dynamic experience called Windows Aero. Both offer a new and intuitive navigation experience that helps you more easily find and organize your applications and files, but Aero goes further by delivering a truly next-generation desktop experience.

Windows Aero builds on the basic Windows Vista user experience and offers Microsoft's best-designed, highest-performing desktop experience. Using Aero requires a PC with compatible graphics adapter and running a Premium or Business edition of Windows Vista.

The following instructions require a computer capable of running Windows Aero, with a default Windows Vista Ultimate installation and student logged in with an Administrator account.

STEPS

- **To Disable Windows Aero**

We recommend that students using this book disable Windows Aero and restore their operating systems default settings (instructions to follow).

1. **Right-click the desktop, select** Personalize, **and then compare your screen in Figure A-10. Select** Window Color and Appearance, **and then select** Open classic appeareance properties for more color options. **In Appearance Settings dialog box, on the Appearance tab, select any non-Aero scheme (such as** Windows Vista Basic **or** Windows Vista Standard**) in the Color Scheme list, and then click OK. Figure A-11 compares Windows Aero to other color schemes. Note that this book uses Windows Vista Basic as the color scheme**

- **To Enable Windows Aero**

1. **Right-click the desktop, and then select** Personalize. **Select** Window Color and Appearance, **then select** Windows Aero **in the Color scheme list, and then click OK in the Appearance Settings dialog box**

FIGURE A-10

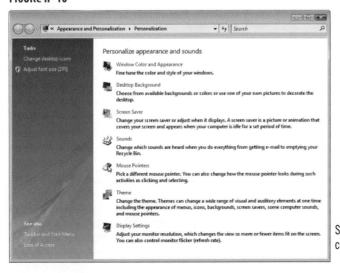

FIGURE A-11

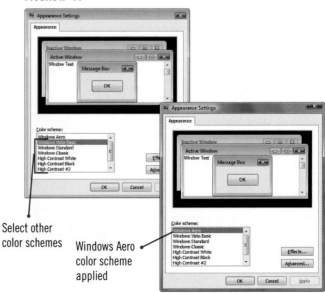

Select other color schemes

Windows Aero color scheme applied

Index